Copyright © 2023 by Jubbery Books

All rights reserved.

No portion of this book may be reproduced in any form without written permission from the publisher or author, except as permitted by U.S. copyright law.

This publication is designed to provide accurate and authoritative information regarding the subject matter covered. It is sold with the understanding that neither the author nor the publisher is engaged in rendering legal, investment, accounting, or other professional services. While the publisher and author have used their best efforts in preparing this book, they make no representations or warranties with respect to the accuracy or completeness of the contents of this book and specifically disclaim any implied warranties of merchantability or fitness for a particular purpose. No warranty may be created or extended by sales representatives or written sales materials. The advice and strategies contained herein may not be suitable for your situation. You should consult with a professional when appropriate. Neither the publisher nor the author shall be liable for any loss of profit or any other commercial damages, including but not limited to special, incidental, consequential, personal, or other damages.

ISBN 978-1-7389114-1-7

# Table of Contents

Chapter 1: Why Grow At Home?
Chapter 2: Planning Your Growing Space
Chapter 3: Garden Examples
Chapter 4: What To Plant
Chapter 5: Garden Layout and Examples
Chapter 6: Tools
Chapter 7: All About Light
Chapter 8: Soil
Chapter 9: Compost
Chapter 10: Fertilizers
Chapter 11: Water
Chapter 12: Germination
Chapter 13: Transplanting
Chapter 14: Mulch
Chapter 15: Companion Gardening
Chapter 16: Care
Chapter 17: Pest Control
Chapter 18: Harvest Time
Chapter 19: Seed Harvesting
Chapter 20: Year End
Chapter 21: Common Mistakes And Solutions
Chapter 22: Growing Guides
Chapter 23: Conclusion
References

# *Garden As Though You Will Live Forever*

—William Kent

"Can you imagine that?"

"What?"

"Being able to garden forever."

"This again? You gave me your 'gardening is glorious' speech last week or have all those fresh vegetables clouded your brain."

"Seriously? When was the last time you were excited to eat a tomato or a carrot?"

"I—"

"You're so bloody busy with your modern city lifestyle that you can't even manage to eat well."

"Hey watch—"

"What, watch you die of malnutrition? At least get a side salad."

"Fine. Go on, explain to me how you're going to turn me into a gardener with a pantry full of preserves."

"You get sick and tired of all that processed food you eat?"

"Ya."

"You know what I eat?"

"Lettuce?"

"Smartass. I eat whatever I want. I have so much food in my apartment I have a different supper every day. If you can tear your device-addicted mind away from your phone for a few minutes, I'll share all my secrets with you. Gardening secrets, that is."

Did you know that humanity eats less than 0.06 percent of the edible plants that grow on the planet? Pretty shocking to think that everyone relies on less than 200 different plants, and three major grains to provide what we eat. As you start to explore the incredible world of growing your own food, I am confident there will be some glorious surprises.

During harvest you get the first real glimpse of what a summer's work can produce, but it is during the cold dark winter that we get to enjoy the previous summer's work: Canned beets at Thanksgiving, zucchini relish and balsamic-tossed canned tomatoes in the New Year, and of course the most amazing pastas and savory tomato sauces whenever the mood hits are just a few of the dishes you can anticipate.

There's a great deal of personal satisfaction for me to open my food storage area and see a year's worth of canned tomatoes, zucchini relish, and pickles of all types just waiting to inspire me. Add to that all the canned peaches, cherries, and pears that were bought at the height of their season and are still bursting with sweet summer memories, the freezer full of peas, carrots, and berries, and I only need to rely on my local grocery store for a fraction of my monthly food.

I can hear your protest that you can't grow anything with your ten black thumbs of death. You may think that is the case, but if you are willing to sit back with your favorite drink as I explain how all this gardening stuff works, you'll be pleasantly surprised at just how simple it all is.

So, settle in and get ready to learn what you need to get started growing amazing food, how to store it over the winter, and how to save on the cost of seeds the next year. The seemingly simple choice to grow your own food will change the rest of your life. Trust me, it changed mine.

# Chapter 1: Why Grow at Home?

This question is really at the root of this book. Why bother taking the time and effort to grow your own food when so much is so readily available?

There are as many reasons people decide to grow their own food as there are people. The most frequent are a desire to save money, eat healthier, and feel a sense of pride in providing for themselves and their families.

You may have other reasons to grow your own food. Perhaps someone once told you that you are unable to, or that it makes no difference where food comes from, or maybe it is as simple as you used to help your parents or grandparents in the garden when you were young. Regardless of why you are starting on this journey I am confident that once you have worked through one cycle of planting a seed to harvesting that produce, and tasting how sweet and satisfying it is you will never feel the same about grocery store produce again.

## Quality

The primary driver for most people is knowing the quality of food they are eating and improving it. When you are responsible for every step in the process from seed selection to harvest you know precisely what has been sprayed or added to your produce. You don't have to rely on the federal food agencies, or even the food companies themselves to be truthful and divulge how they have treated the food.

Think about this statistic for a moment. Vegetables lose 30 percent of their nutrients within three days after harvest. Yes, 30 percent in three days (*Most Produce Loses 30 Percent of Nutrients Three Days after Harvest – Chicago Tribune*, n.d.).

How far is your local grocery store from a potato, lettuce, or carrot farm? I'm going to guess that the nearest farm will be some distance away. The lettuce in your local grocery store will likely have come from California, as that state produces 70% of all the lettuce consumed in the United States.

If you live in New York, your lettuce will have taken about two weeks to get to your local grocery store, and then it may spend an additional day or two in your fridge before you get to it. The Midwest may take a week less, but even California's close neighbor Oregon will still need a few days to get that lettuce from harvest to the grocery store shelf.

These are interesting numbers. The produce that you pay so much for will have already lost a significant amount of its nutritional value before it even reaches your local store.

Once you start growing your own lettuce, the transportation could be as little as ten minutes between harvest, cleaning, and being arranged on your plate. By doing nothing more than growing your own food you are adding some significant amounts of vitamins and minerals to your diet. Not only will this improve your health, but it will also improve your well-being.

## Taste

The soil that your food grows in has a significant impact on the taste of the harvested produce. If you think about the large commercial farms that have no control over their soil other than to add water and fertilizers, you are at a significant advantage over them. You can modify your soil to be the perfect growing medium for your plants and make your produce sweet and nourishing.

We'll get into the details of how to make your soil perfect for your plants in a later chapter, but for now you need to know that the better the match the soil is to the needs of the plants, the better those plants are able to grow. The better the plants can grow, the more produce you will be able to harvest in the fall, and the better this produce will taste.

By knowing local growing conditions, we will cover exactly what this means and how to determine it in a coming chapter, you will be able to select the perfect plants and varieties that will produce the ideal results.

# Environmental Impact

The burgeoning awareness of how far food must travel, the environmental impact of all those truck and ship miles, and the effect this has not only on the taste and quality of the produce, is pushing more people towards farmer's markets and local suppliers.

Produce cannot be more local than if you grow it yourself. The only transportation costs and associated carbon emissions and pollutants are in the effort it takes you to walk out to your garden.

Growing your own food may not make a dent in global carbon emissions, but imagine the impact if everyone on your block, neighborhood, or idealistically your city started growing their own food. How many fewer delivery trucks would be on the road? How much fresher, healthier, and tastier would your food be

# Availability

There is nothing worse than heading to the grocery store for that special ingredient only to find it is out of stock, and the next delivery truck isn't due for another week.

You can only put up with that for so long. Nothing beats the feeling of needing something for dinner and heading to your pantry to find everything you need.

When you plan your garden make sure you are planning around food that you eat. Given the amount of time and effort you will be put into the garden over the summer it would be a shame to have a large harvest of produce that sits unused. Making sure to grow the food that you like and eat will ensure that your pantry is bursting with summer goodness all winter long. And really, at the root of it all is providing your winter food needs. You will learn to tailor your crop to your own requirements

## Cost

As we have been told since we were kids, fresh vegetables are part of a healthy diet. The most sensible approach to this is not working more and more hours at the office so you can afford the painfully expensive produce. Depending on your diet preferences, your location, and how much space you must devote to growing your garden, you might be able to save yourself up to $1,500 per year (*Discover How to Feast Year-Round From a Small Garden!*, n.d.).

## Connection to Nature

The actual act of gardening has been shown to reduce your stress levels, build self-esteem, increase your vitamin D intake, and reduce the chance of heart attacks and coronary diseases (*8 Surprising Health Benefits of Gardening | UNC Health Talk*, 2020).

That sounds like some amazing side benefits from being allowed to go outside and play in the dirt. It seems maybe kids did have something figured out after all.

There is a shift in your view of the world, and how you fit in it once you have grown your own food. The simple act of growing a plant from seed to table reveals the incredible gift we have in the nature that surrounds us.

After a few years of gardening and growing your own food, you will be inspired to change what you eat and how you relate to the world. While you might be an exception, I can say with confidence that all the gardeners that I know have shifted their diets the longer they grow their own food.

This is the beginning of a lifelong journey to discover new plants, how to grow them, and how they taste. Once you have a glimpse of the power of nature, you will be hooked.

# Family Bonding

Do you have memories of working in the garden with your parents or grandparents? What about helping with the fall harvest and canning? If you did not grow up in that type of family, then growing your own garden is an opportunity for you to experience the lifestyle for yourself and share it with your family and loved ones.

As you learn the skills you need to grow your own food, it is the perfect time to involve your family: Maybe give them some radishes to grow, some lettuce to tend, or even their own tomato plant to pick from throughout the summer.

Growing your own food will not only change how you understand food, but it can also be a bonding opportunity: Seed selection, germination, care, harvesting, and preparing the food are all chances to learn something new and create lasting foundational memories with others.

# Chapter 2: Planning Your Growing Space

*"To plant a garden is to believe in tomorrow."*
–Audrey Hepburn

The configuration of your garden will reflect both your location and what you want to grow. Someone with access to a field or other large open space will create a very different type and style of garden compared to someone with access only to an urban backyard, and even more different from what someone living in an apartment will create.

Before we get into the specifics, and examples of garden designs, we are going to touch on how location impacts how much, and what types of plants you can grow.

## Where Do You Live, Big Picture?

### *Climate*

Hot, cold, humid, or dry? There are so many different places to live, and they all have their own local climate. If you live in Anchorage or Haines, then you will have a short growing season to get your crops from seed to harvest. On the other hand, if you live near Miami or Houston, you can typically expect two crops from your garden each year.

Keep this in mind as you look for places to grow your garden. If you are lucky to live somewhere warm, then you can make do with less space than if you are somewhere cold.

The goal is to find a location large enough for all the food you want to grow, and close enough that you are inclined to spend time in the garden.

## Hardiness Zone

In 1927 Dr. Alfred Rehder created a map split into eight regions based on a survey of the plants that grew in each area. This was the initial version of the hardiness maps we know today and the beginnings of an understanding what can and will grow in what areas. The next evolution of the map was done by Dr. Donald Wyman of the Arnold Arboretum in 1938. Instead of using botanical survey results to determine the different growing zones, he used archived data from the US Weather Bureau. He was able to then split the country into many more defined zones without the need to explore every location on foot. These Arnold Arboretum maps were the definitive growing zone maps until 1960.

That's when the US Department of Agriculture (USDA) stepped into the fray and redrew the zone map using data from all the 14,500 weather stations spread across the country. With this single astute move the USDA created the hardiness zone system that has since become the standard in the United States, and now is used in most countries in the world to help classify and manage agriculture and gardening practices.

Hardiness zones give the average minimum temperature of that area, a potential killing factor for plants. It provides no other growing information.

If you are considering planting perennials, they need to be rated to your local zone, or the next coldest one to survive. You will also need to consider the relative humidity the plant needs, the maximum daily temperature it can handle, sun exposure, and water supply.

If you are planting only annuals that will be harvested in the fall, there is little need to worry about the local hardiness zone.

Hardiness zones are divided into fourteen steps, with each one based on the long-term average minimum temperature over the last 15 to 20 years.

## Hardiness Zone Temperatures

| **Zone 0** | -65F, -53.9C | **Zone 5** | -20F, -28.9C | **Zone 10** | 30F, -1C |
|---|---|---|---|---|---|
| **Zone 1** | -60F, -51.1C | **Zone 6** | -10F, -23.3C | **Zone 11** | 40F, 4.4C |
| **Zone 2** | -50F, -45.6C | **Zone 7** | 0F, -17.9C | **Zone 12** | 50F, 10C |
| **Zone 3** | -40F, -40C | **Zone 8** | 10F, -23.3C | **Zone 13** | 60F, 15.6C |
| **Zone 4** | -30F, -34.4C | **Zone 9** | 20F, -6.7C | | |

Hardiness zones vary a great deal across an entire country, but at your specific location you may find that the zone rating varies across your county, state, or even city.

With local micro-climates, wind patterns, and rainfall disparities, hardiness zones are used as a general classification and guide versus a specific growing guide to your backyard garden.

If you are unsure of your hardiness zone, the best source of information is your local garden supply store. They will know if the state level hardiness zone applies, or if the local microclimate is different enough to put your garden in a different zone.

What hardiness zones cannot tell us, is the more important details of the microclimate in your garden. Do you get a lot of wind that will dry out your plants? Are there moisture-rich afternoon winds off the local lake in the afternoon? What about the rain? How much direct sun do you get?

All these considerations will have an impact on what you can grow, how well plants will survive, and if perennials need extra coddling during the winter.

# Canadian Hardiness Zones

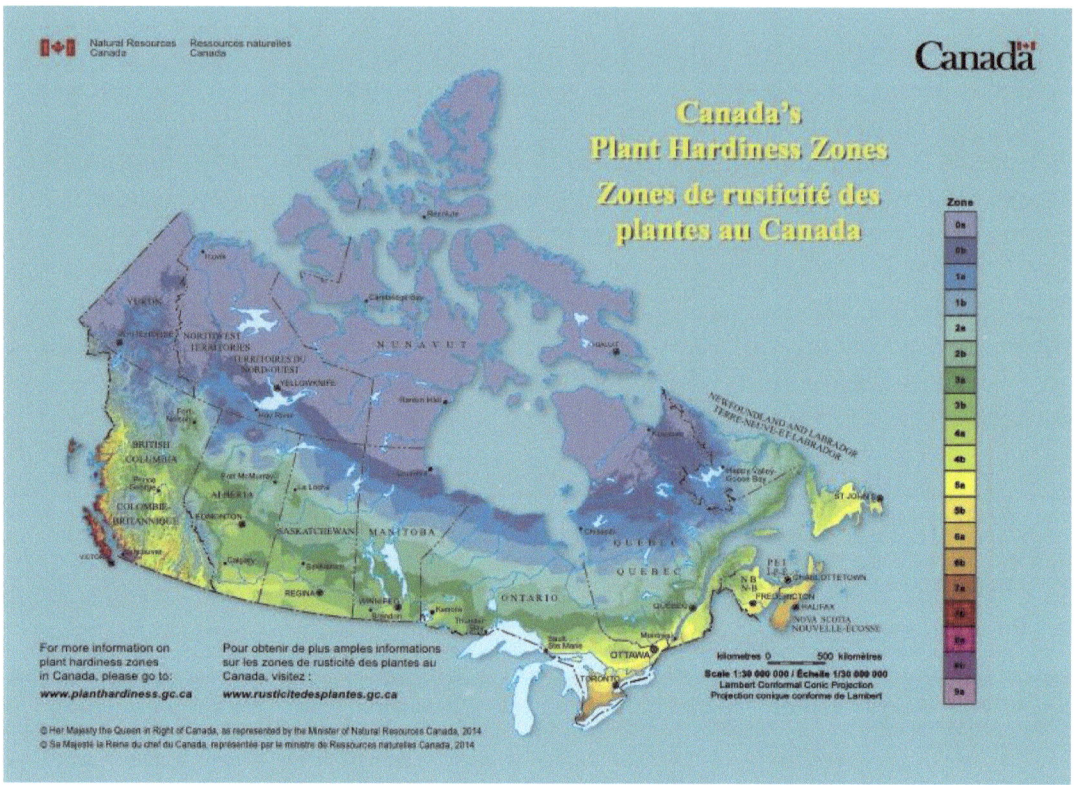

# United States of America Hardiness Zones

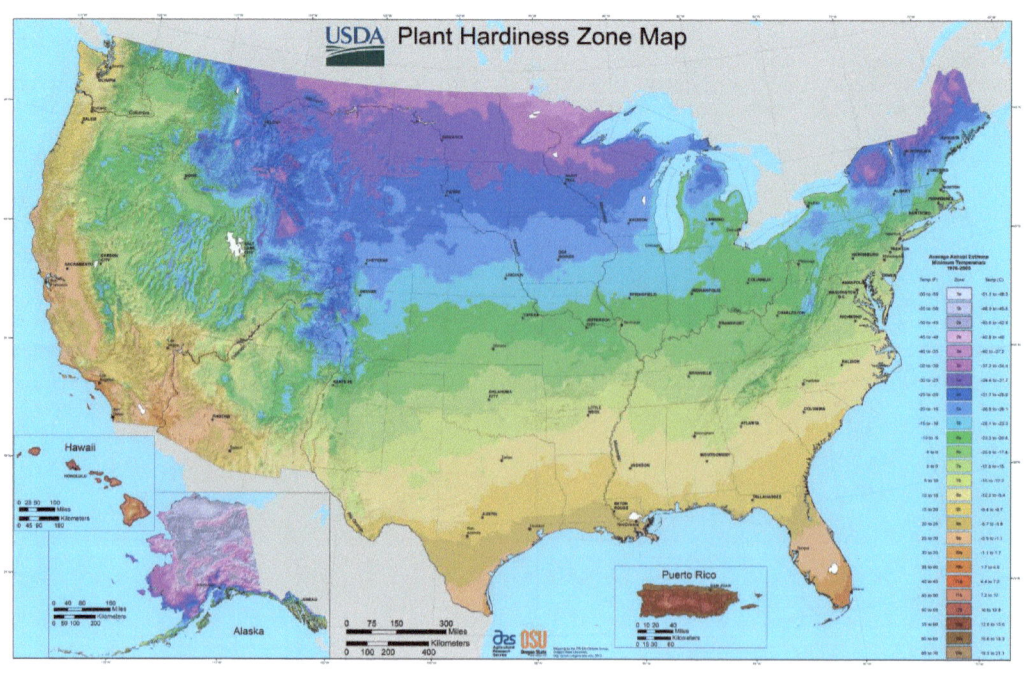

# Chapter 3: Assessing Your Space

*"The glory of gardening: hands in the dirt, head in the sun, heart with nature. To nurture a garden is to feed not just on the body, but the soul."*

— Alfred Austin

## Urban / Suburban House

If, like most of us, you live in an urban area, you will be more restricted on the space you have to use as a garden. Depending on your local housing development, how old it is, and what usage covenants are in place, you may not be able to use as much of your yard as you would like.

For example, it is common in urban areas to not allow vegetable gardening in the front of houses, even though you are allowed to plant non-edible shrubs and trees. Nope, I can't explain that logic either.

Once you know the rules, look around your yard the next time you are outside. Do you get any direct sunlight in your backyard? What about the side yards?

Ideally you are looking for a sunny or bright space to convert into your garden, perhaps some flat open space where you can put a few raised-beds, or even just that sunny corner for a pot or two of herbs or salad greens.

## Apartment / Condo

With an ever-increasing number of people living in apartments and condos, the lack of access to outdoor space to use as a garden has dissuaded many people from even trying to grow their own garden. You may think that you are unable to grow your own food, but you are wrong.

You won't be able to start a market garden from your apartment or condo, but you can easily reduce your food bill by growing all your own leafy greens and vegetables.

If you happen to have a balcony on the sunny side of your building, then growing your own food will be much easier. If your balcony never gets any sunshine, or even if you do not have a balcony, you can still grow some incredible food in railing hung or portable containers.

## Owner / Rental

Obviously, if you own the apartment/condo/house where you live then all the choices regarding setting up your garden are yours to make. If you want to dig up all the grass and put in a garden, then you will only have to answer to your partner or family.

On the other hand, if you rent, you will need to be more careful. Some landlords are open to the idea of setting up a garden, while others will not let you do anything other than mow the grass.

If you live in a rented apartment or condo, you may be restricted to free-standing and non-invasive growing techniques. We will cover all the possibilities in the next section so you can figure out which technique is best.

# Chapter 4: What to Grow

*"It's difficult to think anything but pleasant thoughts while eating a homegrown tomato."*

– Lewis Grizzard

With all this talk about making a garden and growing your own food, we have not yet touched on what you would grow, so let me plant some ideas.

Over the last hundred years or so there has been a rise and fall in the popularity of backyard gardening. With the availability of modern seed catalogs and internet ordering, it is now possible to put together a glimpse of the most common plants grown by home gardeners.

Obviously, the type of plants will vary depending on where you are located, your personal taste, and the amount of land you must work with, but this list can act as a starting point to give you some ideas. Just because you do not see your favorite plant on this list does not mean you cannot grow it. It's just that you may need to do some more research to determine the ideal growing conditions.

- Asparagus
- Basil
- Beans
- Beets
- Broccoli
- Brussel Sprouts
- Cabbage
- Carrots
- Cauliflower
- Celery
- Collard Greens
- Cucumber
- Dill
- Egg Plant
- Garlic
- Kale
- Leek
- Lettuce
- Melon
- Onion
- Okra
- Parsley
- Parsnip
- Peas
- Peppers
- Potato
- Pumpkin
- Radish
- Raspberries
- Rhubarb
- Turnip
- Spinach
- Squash
- Strawberry
- Sweet Corn
- Sweet Potato
- Swiss Chard
- Tomato
- Oregano
- Zucchini

Using this list of common plants, we will look at the typical layout and planting options ranging from a full suburban or urban yard to what you can grow on your apartment balcony or your kitchen counter.

The following table summarizes the common categories of garden plants that can be grown in most typical gardens.

| In The Ground | Raised- Bed | Containers |
|---|---|---|
| Herbs | Herbs | Herbs |
| Leafy Greens | Leafy Greens | Leafy Greens |
| Root Vegetables | Root Vegetables | Limited Root Vegetables |
| Vining Plants | Vining Plants | |
| Brassicas | | |
| Gourds | | |

The type of plants you want to grow will influence the type of garden space you want to create, and vice versa your available garden space may dictate what type of plants you can grow.

Remember that all of these can be mixed and matched to suit your situation. Perhaps you want only raised-bed plots in your backyard because your family loves the grass, but you need more growing space. You can scatter about as many containers as you like and look at hanging a living wall on the fence, or even the wall of your house to add still more growing space.

There is absolutely nothing to stop you from growing a pumpkin patch or corn row in your backyard or spare bedroom, but that might involve more work and costs than anticipated. But who am I to say you can't, perhaps you'll stumble across the next gardening revolution and help feed the world.

# Chapter 5: Garden Options

*"Don't worry about perfection. Nature doesn't grow in straight lines."*

– Lisa Lubell

One of the most successful methods to plan your garden is to consider the foods you like to eat and plant those plants. A simple place to start is with your favorite vegetable soup and salad.

For these dishes you might need to grow tomatoes, celery, onions, parsley, thyme, and garlic. The few remaining ingredients like mushrooms and bay leaves, you can pick up from your local grocer the day before you make the soup.

Using these soup and salad recipes as a starting point, we will look at how the needs of these plants will affect both the garden design and layout.

## In the Ground

Traditionally, gardening has always been in the ground. And if you have the space, this is the least expensive garden set-up. To start your garden in the dirt, all you need is a shovel, seeds, and a watering can or hose. And, of course, do remember that while I'm calling it dirt for now, gardeners prefer to call it soil, if you don't mind.

When you are considering where to put your garden, keep in mind all the other people who use the space, and if your fancy new garden will get in the way.

To create a garden bed in the ground, all you need to do is remove any top cover such as grass, then work the dirt with your shovel until it is clump free and ready for planting your seeds or seedlings. You may also need to consider what soil additives might be required, the specifics of which we will cover in a later chapter.

## Raised-Beds

If you are not ready, or permitted to dig up your lawn or yard then you could look at raised-bed gardening. This is a halfway point between in-the-ground gardening and growing everything in pots.

Using a raised-bed garden is a bit more expensive the first year but will allow you greater control over the soil and thus greater harvests than from growing in the ground.

The quick and dirty definition of raised-bed gardening is using a large container on legs that can be positioned where you want it, or where it needs to be for proper light or water. A bonus is that it can be removed when you are done gardening or change homes.

If you are the handy type, you can build your own raised beds. A quick search online and you will find enough raised-bed options to keep you looking for as long as you like. Just make sure you eventually do choose one, so you can start growing some plants.

When you are considering a raised-bed style garden, it is a good idea to make sure that you have positioned them properly before you fill them with dirt. Once filled, they will be too heavy to move.

## Containers

Another gardening option is to use individual containers, or pots, for each plant. While this might seem expensive initially, if you get decent quality pots, they will last for years. In fact, I have some pots in my personal collection that have outlived several raised-beds and a few house moves.

When you are looking for containers, here are a couple considerations:

The first of these is to find a pot that you like the looks of. Remember, you will be looking at this pot every time you are in your garden. I am pretty sure that the plant will fare much better if you like how the pot looks. Now I am no judge of taste and would never think to tell you what style of pot to use, but keep in mind that these pots may be visible to the public, and not everyone has the same appreciation for wild and crazy pot designs.

Another consideration when you are choosing your pots is to make sure that you can move them about. I know that this seems obvious, but I know many people – myself included unfortunately– who have chosen a pot based on attractiveness only to realize they I needed to call for help every time they wanted to rearrange any plants.

Now if you have better friends than I, who demand pizza and beer every time they help me, it might not be a problem for you. But in my case, after a few months I realized I had spent more on beer and pizza than the pots were worth. Don't get me wrong, it is good to involve your friends in your gardening journey, but you might be able to save a few dollars by buying smaller pots.

If you have only a balcony to convert into a garden space, you may want to investigate railing containers in addition to regular pots. The railing containers are designed to sit on top of the railing with lower sections on each side to keep them stable. Most of these styles of containers are shallow and not suitable for deep root plants like carrots, but they are ideal for salad greens and peppers.

The final few considerations are more on the technical side of growing. Make sure the pots are deep enough for your selected plants. The ideal soil depth can be found in the growing guides. A drip tray is only a concern if you might ever bring the plants inside or to protect the deck your pots are on, but seeing as most pots cost pretty much the same whether they have a drip tray or not, get the ones with the tray.

A last comment on pot choice has to do with the winter weather at your location. If you are going to leave your pots outside all winter, and it gets significantly cold where you live, try to avoid permeable products such as unglazed pottery and concrete. These tend to absorb water during the summer and the cold weather over the winter may crack them.

I am sure there are many other types of containers out in the world that I have no knowledge of, but if it will hold soil, is about the correct depth, and is waterproof than it will work as a place to grow your plants.

Some of the more absurd containers I have run across are kids' inflatable tubs, wheelbarrows, clown sized shoes, unused dresser drawers, kitchen mixing bowls, cowboy hats, and Styrofoam coolers.

Part of the fun of gardening is creating a space that makes you happy to be in, and part of that is letting your creative impulses run wild. If you want to grow your lettuce in a clown shoe, that is fantastic. Your carrots in an old cement mixer? Potatoes in the trunk of a 57 Chevy? Then by all means go out into the world and create a space that makes you happy.

# Allotments / Community Gardens/ Guerilla Gardening

Now, the unfortunate reality is that not everyone has a space to turn into a garden. If you live in an apartment, you will likely not be allowed to tear out the communal grassed area and grow tomatoes. You may also not be allowed to grow in your own living space, with the risk of water damage and the mess created by all the soil, not to mention there may not be enough space or light to grow everything you want.

But don't let these little details discourage you from pursuing your dream. Thankfully, there are a few more options that might work.

Depending on where you live, you might have access to or the ability to gain access to public gardening spaces. Based on the victory gardens that were established during World War II, these public spaces were put aside to allow people to garden who do not have the space.

In my experience, these allotments or community gardens as they are sometimes called, will usually have a waitlist along with a small fee associated with them. Even so, if you are lucky enough to have these in your area, they are worth investigating.

But don't despair if you don't. Some local governments will happily create a garden allotment space if you approach them with the idea. There may need to be a certain number of people involved and for a minimum length of time but consider the value of land and the ability to grow your own food. Even if you must get out and find a few more gardeners who are interested in the same things, in the end you will have a garden space to grow your own food and have met some great people along the way.

Like most people, at some point there is a good chance you will have come across the term "guerilla gardening". And no, this does not refer to getting dressed up in a gorilla suit when you are working with your plants.

It refers to that legally gray area of using public spaces to grow a garden. I have a little exercise for you next time you are out for a walk. I am confident that you have an idea of what you would like to grow, and if you refer to the growing guide section, you will see the suggested plant spacings.

If you do a little math, you will soon come up with a rough idea of the amount of space that you would need. When you walk around your neighborhood, look at the unused spaces around you. The grass verges between the sidewalk and the street, the grassy area beside that apartment tower and the one next door, or even the raggedy planters that sit outside most apartment buildings and manage to support nothing more than a collection of half-dead plants, garbage, and cigarette butts.

Now imagine looking after these locations, fixing up the soil, and suddenly you are looking at a productive and healthy garden where there was nothing more than weeds and garbage.

The obvious problem is that you need to get permission to use those spaces, even though they are nothing more than eyesores that cost the owners money to look after.

This is not without risk. You can plant your seeds and try to look after them, but you are at the mercy of feral animals and people who may help themselves to your produce, as well as the police if the land-owner objects. The flip side is you might just start a local trend and beautify the neighborhood.

Now, I have come across both situations. It seems that if there is a sympathetic local government or landowner and a strong local community, guerilla gardening might be just the thing your neighborhood needs. On the other hand, you might find all your hard work torn up and destroyed.

The choice is yours, so choose wisely but there are times where it might pay off to look beyond your own needs to that of the community, but don't break the law in the process.

## Indoors

The last option left to most people is to simply grow their plants indoors.

As I mentioned earlier, using containers will work both inside and out for growing your plants. The only additional considerations that need to be looked at, when you are planning to grow indoors, are the amount of light that your plants need, and any potential damage from a water leak. You certainly don't want an overwatered plant pot to leak down into the apartment below yours.

When it comes to light, ideally you can put your plants in a location that gets six hours of direct sunlight each day. If you don't happen to live in a south-facing apartment, put your plants where they can get as much light as possible, or investigate options for supplemental lighting.

# Chapter 6: Tools

*"A good tool improves the way you work. A great tool improves the way you think."*

— Jeff Duntemann

Everyone loves a good tool. Well, that may not be universally true, but as you delve into your gardening journey you will develop an appreciation for tools, and not only how they can make your life easier but also how they help you produce more food.

We are going to filter through the endless number of tools on the market and look at the most useful ones that should find a home in your garden shed. As well we will look at how to use these tools as efficiently as possible.

I am sure that we have all seen the infomercials, or YouTube videos that exclaim the incredible properties of some exclusive new-fangled tool that is only available for a limited time. And how for less than a cup of coffee a day, your life will be endlessly improved, oh and it will be so good that we will offer a discount if you buy two of them.

Well, that is all marketing hype aimed at people who do not understand the needs of their gardens. Just as the plants we eat have not changed in any significant way in the last several thousand years, neither have the gardening techniques.

Obviously, we have modern irrigation systems, chemical fertilizers, and even genetically modified organisms (GMO) varieties of our favorite plants that can resist the effects of insecticides and environmental stresses, but we are still responding to the natural cycles and requirements of the plants to help them grow and produce our food.

Now I am not suggesting that we all go out and use stone age obsidian-bladed sickles and wooden hoes to tend our gardens, but more along the lines of understanding the tasks that need to be done and the best tool to accomplish that task.

By dividing the tools into job classifications, I hope to clear away any confusion as to what tool can be used for which job, or jobs. There is no need to fill your garden shed with hundreds of shiny new tools, unless of course you feel the urge to do so. If you are simply focused on the requirements of maintaining and caring for your garden, then you may be pleasantly surprised by how few tools you require.

# Digging

As you need soil to grow your plants in, it makes sense to start with the tools you will need to work with your soil. Shovels come in a seemingly endless number of sizes, shapes, handle styles, and costs. Let's dig into the fascinating world of shovels, starting with their anatomy.

## Grip

Starting at the top you will see either a D-shaped, or just a simple shaft that may have a rounded end. The D-grip is usually made from molded plastic, but some vintage or antique grips may be made from metal. The D shape-grip is commonly found on short-handled shovels to help increase grip and allow the shovel to perform as well as a long-handled version.

## Shaft

The shaft is the long handle section that you hold as you use the shovel. These can be made from metal, fiberglass, wood, or plastic depending on the intended use of the shovel.

A metal shaft is the strongest, heaviest, will last the longest, and is cold to the touch if you do not wear gloves. These are typically used in commercial and industrial locations where aesthetics and useability are secondary to reliability.

A fiberglass-shafted shovel is used typically for working around electricity. It adds an extra layer of protection for the user, as the shaft does not conduct electricity. A fiberglass-shafted shovel is very strong, warm to the touch without gloves, light weight, but expensive.

A plastic-handled shovel is most found in beach play toys and cheap disposable tool sets. Any shovel with a plastic handle should either be hung on the wall of your garden shed or given to your kids to play with. Regardless of what you do with a plastic-handled shovel, keep in mind they are of little use in your garden.

Wooden-handled shovels have been around as long as shovels. They are nearly as strong and reliable as metal or fiberglass. They are light to wield, warm to the touch, long-lived, and easy on your hands.

Now, the heyday of shovel shaft manufacturing is long gone, but a wooden-shafted shovel can provide you with decades of splinter-free use if you look after it. You can find perfectly serviceable wooden handled shovels at most garage or estate sales.

**Length**

When you are choosing a shovel, or making the ones you own more suitable for you, consider all the different tasks that you will be using a shovel. Typically, a long-handled shovel should reach between your elbow and your shoulder when the shovel is held upright, and the point of the blade is just touching the ground.

The lighter the material you will be moving with the shovel, the longer the handle can be. Regardless of what material the shaft/handle is made from, the longer the handle, the more leverage you will have.

**Blades**

The actual business end of a shovel is called the blade. This will come in several different shapes for different uses. While any shovel will move soil, gravel, sand, or snow; if you select the correct blade style and size the material can be moved more efficiently.

Blades that are triangular or round tipped are intended for moving sand and loose dry soil. When you see a shovel with a flat square blade, then you know these are intended for moving large coarse material like gravel. Shovel blades that taper to a sharp point are best used for digging in heavy, dense soil such as clay.

If you are looking for a shovel to do some heavy digging, such as making holes for a new fence post or removing the sod covering part of your backyard, then make sure the shovel blade has a rolled-over top or some other style of flat spot to place your foot. This will not only allow you to put a great deal more pressure on the shovel and remove your material faster, but it will also be much easier on the sole of your foot.

### *So, Which One(s) Do I Need?*

For most common vegetable gardening needs you can easily get by with a long-handled shovel with a rounded blade that comes to a gentle point. This will work well for moving your compost around, mixing up the soil for your plants, as well as general yard clean up in the fall.

If you are laying out garden beds in the ground, then a flat-bladed shovel will make simple work of cutting the edges of the bed straight and help keep the grass and other weeds at bay.

In addition, a small handheld trowel will be helpful for transplanting your seedlings once they are hardened off, removing the root ball after harvest in the fall, and assisting with stubborn weed removal during the summer. When selecting a trowel, make sure that it fits well into your hand, and that the blade is six to eight inches long and tapers to a shallow point.

# Weeding

When you make the perfect growing conditions for your plants, you must know that any other plant that can make a go of it will set down roots in your garden. There are several different techniques that you can use to deal with all these interlopers.

If you are more Zen and relaxed than I am, you will let the weeds grow among your plants and simply let them be.

The more common approach is to pull them out or use a weeding hoe. Start with pulling the weeds by hand—as this is not only very effective but also free. If this is not your cup of tea, then let's look at some tools to help keep your garden weed free.

# Hoe

If you are growing in the ground, and have enough room, use a long-handled hoe. A hoe looks like large flat piece of metal stuck on the end of a shovel handle. By dragging it through the soil, you disturb the roots of the weeds and effectively kill them.

If you are growing in a smaller place, such as a raised bed, you can use a small handheld hoe to work the soil around the stalks of the plants.

# Watering

Everything that you grow in your garden will require water, with some needing more than others.

There are several different approaches to getting water to your plants and each one relates to how much work you are willing to do.

The least effort required to water your plants is to let the rain fall and call it enough. While this may work in humid areas like the tropics, it is less effective in most other areas.

Depending on the size of your garden, you may need to use garden hoses and sprinklers to water all your plants. This approach will work for the standard in-ground garden beds, as a lawn sprinkler will easily satisfy all your plants' needs.

If you are gardening in a raised-bed or containers, you will likely need a watering can. These come in every possible size and design to suit your style. The important considerations are: Does it have a rain shower head to deliver the water without damaging the plants and eroding the soil? Are you able to carry the watering can when it is full of water? Is it simple to fill?

Some watering cans are small with a narrow long arched neck. These have been designed for spot watering of container plants and are typically what you would find with indoor house plants. They are not ideally suited for watering a larger garden setup as the direct water flow will burrow deep into the soil and disturb the plant roots but if you already own this style of watering can, it will be more than adequate for your vegetables if you are careful how you water.

# Care

When it comes to looking after your plants once they are established in your garden, raised bed, or containers, all you really need are your eyes and your fingers. You may find some people who swear that they need a cartload of tools to make sure that all their plants grow properly. But odds are you already have all the tools you need.

# Pruning

Part of looking after your plants during the growing season is to prune them appropriately. When done correctly this will not only encourage lots of growth, but it can also reduce the impact and presence of pests.

You will have likely seen the garden tools displayed at your local garden supply or big box store and the vast array of nippers, scissors, and other cutting tools.

Most of these cutting tools are more suited to landscaping and tree care than vegetable gardening. When you are looking for tools for your garden, you will only need two cutting tools. These will let you do all the pruning and harvesting required during the season.

The first of these cutters is the curved edge secateur. The important aspects of these cutters are a tight-fitting pivot point so that the blade will open and close smoothly and not deflect when you are cutting. When choosing, make sure the handles fit well and the spring is not too strong for your hands.

Once you have purchased your secateur, treat it with care as the curved cutting blade will be extremely sharp. Your secateur is used for pruning thick branches during the growing season and cutting plant stalks once the season is over and you are removing the dead plants in preparation of winter.

The other set of cutters that you should invest in are tomato snips. These have delicate long thin blades used to trim unwanted shoots on tomato plants. They are also perfect for the daily harvest of herbs, ripe tomatoes, and other vegetables.

As with your secateur, the tomato snips are extremely sharp. When you are finished using either of your cutting tools, make sure to wash them so you will not transfer any diseases or small pests, –such as aphids– between your plants. Now, I am not saying that you need to run a medical-grade autoclave to keep your tools ready to use, but you are working with plants that you are going to eat so keep your tools clean.

# Chapter 7: Harvest

## Harvesting

This is what it is all about, right? After all that time hanging out in the summer sun as you care for your plants. All through the summer, you will do your best to keep your plants happy and healthy to encourage them to grow as much produce as possible.

Depending on which plant you are looking at, you may be able to harvest all summer long or you may have only a single harvest at the end of the season. If you are growing herbs, most can be picked as soon as the leaves have matured.

When it comes to basil, oregano, and rosemary you can collect the leaves regularly once the plant has become established in your garden.

The same approach to harvesting applies to most leafy greens as well. Instead of pulling the entire lettuce plant from the garden when you want a salad, use your tomato snips to cut off enough outer leaves to fill your salad bowl. Make sure that you take no more than half of the existing leaves as this will keep the lettuce, spinach, or other leafy green plant alive and ready to be harvested again in a week or so.

Harvesting tomatoes will depend on the type of plant you are growing. If you are growing an indeterminate plant, a plant that does not have predetermined size and will grow until it is unable, then you will likely have tomatoes ready for harvest every week to ten days. Given the productive nature of these plants, it is a good idea to not plant too many unless you want a dozen or more tomatoes every week.

If you have a determinate tomato plant, one that will grow to a predetermined size and then stop, then you will have a single harvest in the fall. Given the differences between these two types of plants, most gardeners will grow the indeterminate plants, such as Roma, for a large fall harvest and several indeterminate plants, such as beefsteak, for a trickle harvest during the summer.

The only tools you need, besides an understanding of when the produce is ripe and ready to be picked, is a handy basket for all your treasures and your tomato snips. Unless it is the end of the season you should pick only what is ripe and for your immediate use. The produce will last much longer on the plant than it will in your fridge.

## Preserving

Harvesting your garden bounty during the summer should supply you with enough fresh food for all your needs, and if there happens to be an excess of tomatoes every now and then, you can use the excess for a Greek salad or tomato on toast.

When it comes to the final harvest in the fall you will need a plan to manage all the produce that will suddenly appear in your kitchen.

Most everyone has heard about canning garden produce, as well as dehydrating, smoking, and pickling. We will quickly cover the common tools for each of these food preservation techniques.

### Canning

There are two different techniques for canning depending on what fruit or vegetables you want to preserve.

#### Water Bath

This is the most common type of canning. If you have childhood memories of the pot of steaming water on the stove, all the glass jars with their two-piece lids, and the snap and pop as the lids sealed, then you are remembering water-bath canning. The fundamentals of this technique are a large pot of boiling water, the individual jars packed with the fruit and vegetables in a syrup or brine of some sort. When the jars are put in the boiling water, the liquid inside the jar comes to boil and sterilizes the inside of the jar, if the filled jars are processed for more than twenty minutes. If the processing time is less than this, then the jars will need to be sterilized prior to filling. The syrup or brine that the produce is in will help reduce the growth of detrimental bacteria.

The lifespan of water-bathed produce is one year. The jar may remain sealed for much longer than this but because water bath canning is unable to kill all the bacteria in the jar, the longer the food is on the shelf the greater the chance of botulism or other toxic bacteria growing.

To ensure all your food is processed correctly for safe storage, follow the manufacturers recommendations that comes with your canning jars and related products.

**Pressure Canning**

This operates on the same principle as the water bath canning, but the high pressure and temperature can kill most of the bacteria in the food and the jar.

If you are looking to preserve tomatoes, you need to use a pressure canner. The modern tomato varieties do not have the low pH that made water-bath canning of tomatoes safe for your grandparents. The additional pressure of the pressure canner will ensure that not only will the produce be safe to eat but will also extend the life of the preserved food from one year to five years. Don't consume home-canned produce that is more than five years old, or any commercial produce that is more than ten years old (University, n.d.).

*Dehydrating*

Tea, homemade spices, and sundried tomatoes are just a few of the products you can create from your fall harvest.

You can dehydrate food in a dehydrator that can fit on your countertop. By following the instructions for your model of dehydrator, you will be able to ensure that the final product is dried enough to be safely stored.

If your kitchen oven can hold a low enough temperature to dry out the food and not cook it, between 120 and 160 Fahrenheit, then you could use it in place of a dehydrator.

If you live in a warm climate or have harvested your produce early in the season, you can also dry your produce in the sunshine. This is the traditional Mediterranean method to preserve herbs and tomatoes.

To do this you will need a sunny, well-ventilated area. Make sure to wrap your produce in cheesecloth to keep the flies and other insects from contaminating your food. If your location gets an evening dew, place the items under cover or bring them inside at night.

When your produce is fully dried it cracks and breaks when you fold it in half. It is then ready to store.

### *Pickling*

Most commonly, you will find that cucumbers are pickled, but you can also pickle carrots, beets, potatoes, zucchini relish and pretty much any other type of vegetable that you fancy.

With pickling vinegar and spices to suit your taste, fill the jars with your produce and top up with brine. Place in your fridge and wait a week if you can, and then enjoy.

### *Freezing*

If you do not want the complexity and work of the other preservation techniques, you can simply put your harvest in your freezer. Keep in mind that some vegetables like peas will need to be partially cooked (blanched) before freezing, spaced apart on cookie sheets, to preserve the best texture and flavor.

Most frozen vegetables and herbs will retain their nutritional value but will lose texture. Frozen vegetables are best used in soups and stews.

### *Cold Room*

The easiest method to preserve produce is to store it in a cold dark place until you are ready to use it. This can be in the fridge if you have the room, a spare fridge if you do not, or in an old-fashioned cold room that is vented to the outside and unheated but kept above freezing. As most people do not have a cold room in their basement, nor willing to install one, the most common approach is to buy a new fridge and use the old one for vegetable storage. The one drawback is the lack of ventilation in the storage fridge. To overcome this, you store your produce in vented containers, open, and rearrange the fridge every couple weeks to remove any excess humidity.

# Chapter 8: All About Light

*"Dawn is the time when nothing breathes, the hour of silence. Everything is transfixed, only the light moves."*
— Leonora Carrington

Sunlight can warm you on a cold winter day, scorch you on a summer day, and tan you when you are lounging about. It also grows all our food. Without the sun there would be no plants and without plants to feed us we would not be here.

But a sunny day is not the same for us as it is for your plants. A bright and lovely summer's day is the source of many of our dreams, but that same idyllic day might be too bright, too dim, or if you are lucky, provide just the right amount of sunlight for your garden.

## What is light?

What we see as sunlight, is only a miniscule portion of the spectrum of energy emitted from the sun. This energy is part of what is known as the electromagnetic (EM) spectrum. The EM spectrum encompasses the radio signals you listen to, the microwaves that reheat your cup of coffee, the infra-red that allows the military to see at night, and helpfully, the sunlight that powers both our summer dreams as well as our gardens (*Electromagnetic Spectrum - Introduction*, n.d.).

This EM energy is divided into segments by a range of wavelengths. If we use microwaves, the full afternoon sun on a sunny day, and radio waves as examples, we find that microwaves have such tightly packed waves that they can pass right through some objects and heat them up in the process. It was the discovery of a pocket full of melted chocolate in 1945 that led to the discovery of the microwave oven (celcook, 2017).

When we then look at the properties of radio waves, we see that these waves are much wider spaced, and because of this, they can bounce off buildings, different layers in the atmosphere, and even off the surface of lakes and rivers if the conditions are right.

In between these two examples is where we find sunlight. Sunlight is not small enough to pass through our bodies like microwaves, nor does it bounce off buildings like radio waves, but it is the fuel that powers all life on our planet. All you need to do is to stand out in the summer sun and you can feel it warming you from the outside in.

Sunlight feeds your plants through a process called photosynthesis. By using the water drawn up by the roots, the carbon dioxide in the air, and the energy from the sun, plants combine and transform these fundamental components into sugar and oxygen (*What Is Photosynthesis |*, n.d.).

## How much is enough?

How much light do your plants need? The simple answer is that it depends. Just like people, some plants love baking in the bright afternoon sun while others are very happy to relax in the shade.

When you buy your seeds, the package will typically have growing instructions on the back that includes information about the plant size, spacing, and how much sunlight the plant prefers. This will fall into one of three categories.

The first one is full sunlight. This is what it sounds like, your plant wants to be in the full glare of the sun. It wants that golden summer tan, that afternoon sweat, and that bleach blonde hair. These plants will survive in less than the full sun but will complain and pout while being less productive than they could be.

Partial sun or partial shade will be the next most common light preference. Again, this is what it sounds like. Plants in this category will grow well in a location that receives a few hours of bright direct sunlight in the morning or afternoon and spends the rest of the day in a brightly lit but shaded area.

The final option on the seed package will say something along the line of shade tolerant, full shade, or shade requiring. Now this does not mean you can put this plant under the stairs behind the garbage cans. It won't like that very much at all. A shade requiring plant still needs the bright daylight but shouldn't be exposed to the glare of the direct sunlight. If your garden location makes it difficult to find a shaded area, you can hang shade cloth or find something they can grow under and be protected from the harsh sunlight.

# Chapter 9: Soil

*"Fertility of the soil is the future of civilization."*
— Albert Howard

Remember that last black-tie gala you attended at the embassy? Did you ever wonder how many gardeners were hidden in that polite and elegant crowd? Just imagine how much easier all that small talk would have been if you knew you had something so interesting in common.

But there is no need to worry. The next time you find yourself debating the state of the food supply chains, the current socio-economic models that perpetuate these systems, and the quality of the pale vegetables in the appetizers served by the circling waitstaff, all you need do is casually wonder outload how mistreated the garden soil must have been to produce such anemic specimens.

If you are beside a gardener, they'll share your wonderment and voila, the door is open for you to shine. However, often, they will simply shrug and utter some meaningless tripe about modern factory farming techniques. This is your queue to look at your glass and be suddenly surprised that somehow your cocktail has been drained without your consent and you really must be excused so you can go look for the culprit, as such flagrant drink abuse should never be tolerated at such a classy event.

Now, yes this might be little more than a "007" inspired flight of fancy, but it does give you an idea of just how important soil can be. To the extent that you would even break character to discuss soil aeration and water retention at an embassy gala.

We are surrounded by dirt whether we like it or not. It is on our shoes, covers our cars, and makes a mess of our clean houses. Call it dirt, mud, ground, or even the land; it makes little difference. Dirt is messy and best left outside.

But now that you are going to grow your own food, dirt has unknowingly become your new best friend. Well maybe not quite yet, but you will become obsessed with it once you understand the importance it has to your plants, and thus your harvest in the fall.

Anyone that has been gardening for longer than an afternoon will politely inform you that you mean soil. Gardeners use soil, construction workers use dirt. After they are satisfied you understand the significance of soil, they are likely to embark on a long monologue on how they manage their soil, why these matters, and why you should stop whatever you are currently doing and follow their process.

## Soil or Dirt?

So, what is the difference, and why make the distinction? The simple answer is that dirt is left the way it has been formed, and things happen to it. Buildings are dug down into it, parking lots paved over top of it, and kids roll about in it whilst laughing. Soil, on the other hand, is a modification of the dirt.

Another way to look at it is soil is dirt that has been made more suited to growth. Obviously, dirt is already ideal for some plants to grow in. Just look at all the farmland across the country, the natural forests, and those creature-infested jungles in the nice warm areas of the globe.

The problems arise as a home gardener you are unlikely to have the luxury of being able to select a different location to put your garden. So, this leaves us in the situation of needing to modify the existing dirt, whether that is coming from your backyard or if you are buying bags or by truckload.

Before we dig into the specific aspects of dirt that are modified to create good soil, you need to know the characteristics of your dirt. We need to have a quick chat about topsoil.

What is topsoil? It is another one of those definitions that is exactly what you would expect it to mean. Topsoil is simply the top layer of the dirt in your yard. It is in this top layer where all the rotting and composting of last year's growth happens, where most of the insect activity is, as well as where you will find almost all the nutrients and minerals that your plants will use as they grow.

The quality of the typical topsoil in a city lot leaves much to be desired if you are a gardener. It is the responsibility of the homeowner to replace this fill and other low-grade dirt. With the cost of good clean topsoil running more than $300 a cubic yard, most developers typically use the excavated dirt and clay that came out of the foundation hole as topsoil. If you have a particularly good builder, they may take advantage of the incredible tenacity of fescue and scatter a few handfuls of seeds about the place and call it a lawn, but this is the exception.

A few months later when the house is on the market, and the realtor has finally handed you the keys, you can be forgiven for thinking your yard is covered in a high-grade topsoil. But this is nothing more than a well-crafted illusion.

If your newly built house did not come with a lawn, your yard will likely have nothing more than a few years of composted weed growth masquerading as topsoil. Either way you look at it, the topsoil that is supporting your vibrant green lawn is typically no more than a couple of inches deep.

The other side of the great topsoil debate, which I may exaggerate a bit to make a point, is that you never know what is hidden beneath that smooth carpet of grass. If your house has been around for a few years, odds are not in your favor.

I am going to share a few words of wisdom from an old farmer I knew. We were leaning up against the side of his truck and chatting. He paused and looked at me, then over at a crooked old aspen tree.

"You're one of those environmental types?" He squinted at me.

I nodded, curious where this was going.

"See that old tree? Proves your wrong."

"What?"

He nodded for me to follow as he ambled across the yard.

"There. Trees still strong and healthy. Dad started that pile some 50 years ago."

I stared at the black mound of used oil filters up to my waist and wider than I could reach, lost for words.

My point with this ramble is what we see as normal stewardship of the land today was not common practice for the previous generations.

What about the old fuel oil drum that fed the furnace? You know the one usually bolted to the side of the house or buried in the backyard. Did it leak?

The thing with the topsoil in your backyard is that unless you go to the time, hassle, and expense to get it tested at a lab, you have no idea what has been done to it and how it might be contaminated. The long and short of the soil in your yard, is that while it will support a lawn, it may not be the best choice to use for your vegetable garden – unless you have no other options.

# Make up of soil.

So, at this stage there is no difference between dirt and soil other than their names and intended use. When you kick the ground with your boot or dig up a section of your lawn and see the dirt underneath, you may see that it is not a singular lump of material but a mix of different materials, unless you are unfortunate enough to have a house built on clay. If this is the case, you will most definitely need to bring in all your garden soil.

## *Types of soils*

Soil can be classified into four basic groups; sandy, silty, loamy, or clay based. That all sounds pretty good and interesting but what does all that really mean?

## Sandy

As you would expect from the name, sandy soil is made up from weathered rocks, also known as sand. The inability of this type of soil to retain any significant amounts of nutrients and minerals, along with the very high drainage rate, make it unsuited for most plants. How many plants did you see growing in the sand the last time you went to the beach? Not many I am guessing.

## Silty

Silty soil is the midway point between sandy and clay-based soils. Silty soil is usually smooth to the touch and will hold water better than sandy soil. Silty soils are normally found near water bodies and more fertile than the other types of soil.

## Clay

Clay based soils are usually so dense that there is little to no water drainage. This type of soil does not create a very good growing environment for your plants and will require extensive modification to make it suitable.

## Loamy

Loamy soil combines all the benefits of all the soil types, the silt soil nutrients, the water retention of the clay, and the aeration of the sandy soils. This is the type of soil we will be aiming to create.

### *Ideal Soil Composition*

The best soil for your plants needs to be a mixture of air, water, minerals, and organic material. The typical soil mixture is 45% minerals, 5% organic matter, 20 - 30% water, and 20-30% air (*Soil Management*, n.d.).

It is by manipulating these ratios that you can adjust your soil to match the needs of your plants. If you are looking to be growing in raised beds or containers, then you can take advantage of the excellent bagged soils that are available at your local garden supply store to remove all the work of modifying your soil.

# How To Make Soil Better

So how do you know what needs to be changed from your existing soil? The only way to be certain is to analyze your soil, with your hands, eyes, and a couple lab tests.

The easiest test you do is to simply grab a handful of soil and squeeze it into a ball. If it crumbles away when you open your hand, then your soil is quite sandy, and you may need to add some clay and organic matter. If your fistful of soil is now a dense lump as hard as a frozen treat on a stick, then it is high in clay, and you will need to add some sand or other aerating additives to it.

When you open your hand, your soil should hold its shape, just. If you shake your hand a bit, it should start to crumble around the edge but overall keep the shape it started with. If you are lucky enough to have soil of this consistency, then you are ready to test for moisture retention and pH, more on pH in a following chapter. The rest of us will now need to figure out what to do with the dirt in our hands.

## *Additives*

The primary concern with the heavy clay soil is to get it to drain. This may come as a surprise. I know I was surprised to learn that you can drown a plant. Other than by throwing it into a lake or river, that is.

If there is too much water sitting around the roots of a plant, there will be no opportunity for the roots to absorb oxygen and help keep the fine hairs on the roots alive and able to extract the nutrients and minerals from the soil. The roots will eventually become waterlogged, start to rot, and die.

A soil made up predominantly of clay will not allow the water to drain. As mentioned before, we need to add something to create some air spaces in the soil to not only provide the air the roots need, but also a path to allow all that excess water to drain.

If you happen to live near a public sand pit, this will work as a great aeration additive to your soil, if you don't mind all the heavy and slow mixing. Next time you think about shoveling and mixing clay, remember how painfully heavy it is and difficult to work with. So, what can you add if you are not built like a medieval blacksmith?

### Peat Moss

The most common additive over the last few generations has been peat moss. This amazing material will add both aeration and organic matter. Depending on the amount of peat moss added, there may even be a change in the pH of the soil. That sounds pretty good to me, but there are some drawbacks.

The most common argument against using peat moss is that it is not a renewable or sustainable product. It comes from the ancient peat bogs and while it could be regenerated, the process takes many centuries.

The second drawback to peat moss is the possible introduction of non-native plants and insects. As we develop the planet more and more each year, we realize the damage that non-native species can do to environments not prepared for them.

If there are no other alternatives available at your location and you do not want to spend the lifetime developing the muscles required to mix enough sandy soil, then peat moss is an option. However, you must weigh the environmental cost of using such a product against the yield from your garden.

## Vermiculite

Another common soil additive is vermiculite. Adding vermiculite to your soil helps with water retention. It also creates voids in soil to help with drainage if you have a heavy clay. There are no nutrients or minerals added to the soil with the vermiculite and the soil pH will remain relatively unchanged.

## Perlite

Another common soil additive is perlite. If you have ever looked at a bag of commercially available soil and noticed all those small white chunks in the soil, then you have already seen perlite.

Perlite is made from volcanic glass which is run through a hot oven. The moisture inside the glass rapidly expands and creates the distinctive white porous material known as perlite.

While not a renewable resource, perlite is sterile after being created and will reduce the likelihood of any unwanted diseases or pests being introduced into your garden.

This matrix is ideal for holding moisture until the plant roots are ready to absorb it. If you have sandy soil, it can hold a great deal of air for the roots to access, it also creates ideal drainage pathways for extra water in clay heavy soils. Adding perlite to your soil will not add any nutrients, minerals, nor affect the pH, if perlite was a renewable resource, it would be the ideal soil additive.

## Coco Coir

The last of the common soil additives is coco coir. This is made from the fibrous outer layer of coconuts and is a by-product of the coconut processing industry. Coco coir is a renewable resource and can be sterilized during part of the production process to keep most unwanted diseases and pests at bay.

When you mix coco coir into your soil, you are getting the benefit of the extra water absorption of the coconut husk fibers. If you have sandy soil, these fibers expand and contract with the changes in moisture content allowing greater soil aeration. These fibers will slowly degrade over time and compost into the soil, adding their nutritional and mineral content like a slow-release fertilizer.

## Other Materials

There are many people who have tried different materials to try to modify their soil to make it more suitable for growing, but there is not enough space in this book to even begin to cover all these possibilities.

If you feel that you have a better material that you can use to modify your soil, there are a couple aspects to keep in mind before you start adding it by the shovel full. Firstly, is there the possibility that you may introduce pests or diseases into your garden? If so, that material choice may cause more problems that it fixes.

Secondly, how will this new material affect the chemistry and pH of the soil? While plants can grow in a wide range of soil conditions, they will perform the best in only a narrow range, and if you are growing the plants for food, you will want them healthy and growing at their best.

Thirdly, it is important to know if this material presents any possible harm to you as the gardener, as well as to you, the produce consumer. It is not uncommon for plants to absorb some of the components of the materials in the soil, in fact, this is what gives the different tastes to the same produce grown in different gardens.

The final consideration for soil additives is cost. Will using that material result in the harvested produce costing more than if you had simply gone down to the local grocery store and bought it?

If you are satisfied with your soil additive over all these concerns, it might be worth trying a small test bed to see how effective it is.

## Soil pH and other Analysis

When you have all the soil additives mixed in and you feel that the soil is ready to be used, the last thing you should do is a pH test. This will give you an idea if you need to adjust it to better suit the plants you plan to grow.

Most plants grow the best if the pH of the soil is somewhere between 6.0 and 7.5. If you refer to the growing guides near the end of the book, you can find the ideal pH range for all your plants.

The pH of your soil can easily be adjusted either up or down as needed.

## *pH Testing*

So, you have all your soil ready to go, and know that you need to test the pH, so how do you do that?

As with most things in life, there are several possibilities depending on your budget. The easiest way to test your soil is to hire a company to take samples, run tests, and send you back a lovely full color report giving you all the nitty gritty details of your soil.

If you can afford this approach, you will have an excellent starting point to customize the soil for your plants. The report will usually have the soil pH, nitrogen, phosphorus, potassium levels, sulfur and boron levels, a breakdown of the type of soil and approximate percentages of sand, clay and silt, a water retention test to indicate how well your soil drains, the presence of common toxins, such as arsenic and lead, as well as the physical structure, composition, and nutrient profile of each sample.

A thorough test like this would immediately spot any of that old oil that may have been dumped on the ground and will give you some peace of mind if you are planning to grow your garden in the ground without the support and benefits of a raised bed.

As you will no doubt expect, testing this thorough is not cheap. Obviously, these numbers will change over time, but current pricing at the time this book was written suggests that you might get enough change from $10,000 to buy a cup of coffee or two.

The steep price of these tests makes them beyond the reach of most people. The other option is a basic pH test that will tell you only the pH of your soil. This is important to the health of your plants and a good starting point.

There are soil specific pH tests that will guide you through the process of collecting a sample of soil, adding enough water to create very runny mud, add different reagents, and analyzing the resultant concoction. These soil pH testing kits do work and can be found typically for less than fifty bucks.

With the broad range of pH values that your plants can grow in, you do not need to be accurate to the tenth of a percentage, just in the ballpark, or even just the same neighborhood. If your test results are within half a pH level up or down of what your plants prefer, that is close enough.

The pH of your soil will change during the growing season. Any rainwater your soil gets will lower the pH to around 6. The city water you will most likely use will bring the pH to 7. Decomposition of the soil and any other organic matter will also move the pH up or down.

You might be wondering what the extreme levels of pH will do to your plants. It is not pretty. If your pH is too low, the soil is more and more acidic. As the numbers drop, your plants will become sickly and droop. If the pH is not increased, the plants will die. When you pull the dead stalks, you will notice the roots will be almost gone. The acid in the soil has literally burned off the roots and without roots, the plants die.

On the other hand, if your plants are dying and you pull the dead stalks out of the soil to find there are plenty of large roots still attached, the soil pH is too high. High pH blocks the uptake of nutrients, minerals, and water through the roots.

If the soil pH is only a little outside the ideal range for your plants, they will survive but might be stunted. Come the fall you will have a much-reduced harvest. Once you have a couple years' experience, you will know whether a plant is stunted or not.

# Chapter 10: Compost

"The longer I live the greater is my respect for manure in all its forms."

— Elizabeth von Arnim

Now, anyone who has spent time around gardeners will have heard about compost. Known to some as black gold, compost can add a great deal of performance to your soil if it is done correctly.

You might have been told that all you need to do is put your dinner and kitchen scraps in a container either under the sink or on the counter and wait until it has rotted. You can then simply mix it into your garden and your plants will magically burst out of the soil. There will be so much harvestable produce that you won't know what to do with it all.

I know that sounds pretty good to me as well, but before you go buy that overpriced bin from the garden store and start filling it with everything out of your fridge, there are a few things we need to know.

To start with, compost, while very good for your soil, is not a magic fix-all. In the most basic of terms, you are transforming the nutrients, minerals, and organic matter in your scrap food into a composition that your garden plants can absorb. These added nutrients and minerals work best when they complement the existing soil.

You may have heard the term hot compost. This refers to both the heat given off as the composting material rots, as well as the amount of nutrients in the rotted material. Let's start with the temperature.

When a compost pile is rotting and transforming all your scraps into usable fertilizer, heat is generated by the microbial activity inside the pile. A well-constructed compost pile will rapidly heat to between 40 and 50 degrees Celsius (100 to 125 F) in the first few days. It is this high heat that will kill off most pathogens and pests and make sure that the finished product is safe for your garden. The heating of the compost will gradually taper off. When it is back to the ambient temperature of the surroundings, then most of the decomposition has been completed. At this stage the compost can be used in your garden, or you can continue to add more material and keep the process going.

Professional composting facilities have large thermometers they can use to probe into the heart of the compost pile to determine when it has cooled enough to be used, but for the typical gardener it is much easier to simply push your hand into the compost and see how hot it is. Do this carefully if the pile is still actively composting in the core. It could be uncomfortably warm. If you live in a cold climate, your compost pile may generate steam as the air temperature drops overnight and if it gets cold enough it will fall dormant until the temperature rises again.

If you plan to compost, it is considered best practice to start with on and start another one whenever the first one has filled the container or location you are using. Research at Cornell University suggests that to be effective, your compost container or pile needs to be a minimum of 10 gallons. This size will allow adequate heat to be retained to keep the compost reactions continuing. If the compost pile is allowed to cool to the ambient air temperature before all the material has been transformed, then the microbes will die off and the process will not be complete.

Along with keeping the compost at the correct temperature, it is also critical that the moisture content of the pile be above 30 percent and below 65 percent. The same Cornell study found that microbial activity is drastically reduced when the moisture content gets too high or low. To help understand just how much moisture is in your compost, there is a squeeze test that will give you some guidance.

If you want to use gloves, go right ahead. All you need do is grab a handful of compost and squeeze it into a ball. If water drips or runs out, then you have too much moisture in your compost. The ideal texture in your hand will be that of a damp but not soaked sponge.

To adjust the moisture in your compost, either water or add juicy scraps such as salad greens and fruit scraps. If it is too wet, add some newspaper or other shredded paper products.

Once you have adjusted the moisture content, you will need to mix all the compost together. Let the compost sit for a day and retest the moisture levels to see if it needs further adjusting. After you do this a few times you will be able to get a good indication of the moisture level just by looking at it when you mix it up every week or so.

If your compost piles are in the yard and you find it is continually too wet, it might make sense to cover it with a tarp to reduce the amount of rain getting in it. The opposite is true if your compost is on the dry side. Create a depression in the top to help hold water until it can be absorbed. You might even look at moving your compost to a more exposed location where it gets more rain.

By having at least two piles or containers for composting, you can continue to create new compost from your food scraps and garden waste while allowing the existing ones to finish their transformation into soil.

Now on to the second meaning of a hot compost, referring to compost that is high in nitrogen and other nutrients. While this might seem like a good thing on the surface, as more is usually better, this is not the case with fertilizers. Yes, just like people, some plants need more nutrients than others, but without very expensive lab tests and equipment there is no way to know exactly the nutrient levels in the compost. It is easier on the plants if you play it safe and make sure that your compost is fully created before you use it. You can always top-dress your tomatoes with another shovel full of compost if they are looking a little pale and anemic.

There are three indicators that your compost is ready for use. The first is that your compost is no longer hot or producing any heat. This is a sign that all microbial activity has slowed down and the material is ready.

Secondly, if your compost is cool to the touch but still contains recognizable food scraps, it has stalled and is not fit to use yet. If this is the case, you need to add more food scraps, some water, and top that off with some dry grass or leaves. This will trap the moisture and scrap together and kickstart the composting again.

Finally, if you look at your compost and it is cool to the touch and looks like a moist black soil, you are in luck. It is pretty much ready to use. Most composts are ready for the garden when their volume has been reduced to half or less of where it started.

# What Can Go in My Compost

By now I am sure that you are wondering just what can be put in your compost and what cannot. A common misunderstanding is that if you eat it, it can be composted. While this is broadly true, there are some exceptions.

- **Ideally suited for composting**
    - All non-meat-based food waste
    - Used coffee grounds and tea, including the teabags and most coffee filters.
    - All vegetable and fruit skins, cores, and other trimmings
    - Eggshells, though these may take several years to compost if they are not broken into small pieces first.
    - Lawn clippings and other plant-based yard pruning and waste
- **Should only be added in limited amounts.**
    - Napkins, paper plates, and other paper-based food containers
    - Newspaper
    - Magazines and books will take many years to compost unless they are shredded.
    - Large branches or logs need to be chipped first.
- **Never put in your compost**
    - Plastic
    - Glass
    - Metal
    - Styrofoam
    - Oil or fat-soaked items
    - Meat
    - Dairy products

This might sound like an onerous list to adhere to, but it can be simplified by seeing it as anything that can be recycled is not allowed, as well as any biodegradable product larger than your thumb.

Meat and dairy products will eventually compost, but before then, they may attract pests and vermin that will cause more harm and damage than the cost of disposing properly of all the meat and dairy you put in the compost.

# Manure

The challenge when starting a garden is that most compost will need at least a full season to rot and mellow enough to be of any use to your plants. Your first gardening season is, unfortunately, usually the most expensive as you have not had the time to create your good soil and must purchase all the additives and compost materials.

So, when you go to the garden store you will have likely seen all those bags of soil and compost usually outside the main doors, or somewhere else just as visible. These are marketed as compost for gardeners who maybe do not want to create their own, have no space, or are new to gardening and have not yet learned to make their own.

These bags of soil and manure have a place in vegetable gardening. It is important that you know the differences between all the available products, so you use them as they are intended.

Manures are generally classified as either hot or cool. Now, this has nothing to do with their temperature, but where the organic material comes from to produce the manure, and the resulting levels of nutrients and minerals.

If the manure is from omnivores or carnivores, such as chickens or pigs, the manure is considered hot. If there are no labels on the bags, you can identify a hot manure from a cold one by odor and texture. A hot manure will have a strong odor and a slimy appearance.

As you may have already guessed, a cold manure comes from herbivores such as cows and horses. This type of manure has a milder odor, is crumbly, and drier.

I can hear you wondering why does this matter? Well, the type of manure will have a direct impact on how you can use it without damaging your plants. If you bring home a bag of hot manure, then you need to let it sit and age for a season to lower the nutrient levels, so it doesn't harm your plants.

If you select a cool manure, such as one from sheep or horses, you can mix it in with your topsoil to add those nutrients and minerals for the current growing season.

If you want to add some compost to your soil, you should understand the most common types of manure.

- Chicken Manure
    - Very high in nitrogen and phosphorus
    - Must be aged for at least one season before using.
    - When adding to your compost pile, add one portion of chicken manure to every four portions of dry vegetable matter such as hay, dried leaves, or shredded paper.
- Horse Manure
    - High nitrogen levels
    - When dry, it can be applied to the soil with one part horse manure to twenty parts soil.
    - Ensure that it has been aged at least one year to kill off any weed seeds that may have passed through the horse.
- Cow Manure
    - Lower in nitrogen than horse or chicken manure
    - Once it has aged for a year, cow manure can be added to the soil with one part cow manure to twenty parts soil.
- Sheep Manure
    - Lower nitrogen levels but good levels of potash
    - Acts more like a slow-release fertilizer than most other manures.
    - Add to your soil the same as horse manure.

As with most things in life, when there are many options available, there are usually recommendations as to when to use each option. The same is true for manures.

If you are primarily growing leafy greens, root crops, and other vegetables, it is recommended you primarily use correctly aged chicken, cow, or horse-based manures. These will provide the best balance of nutrients and minerals, particularly if you are unsure of the specific composition of your soil.

You may run across other types of manures at your local garden supply store depending on what is locally available but before you purchase and spread it all through your garden, I suggest you have a quick chat with the store staff. They can recommend the best solution suited for your application.

# How To Compost

We alluded previously that you need to add more wet items or dry items to manage the moisture levels in your compost. But what else is involved with creating a successful compost?

You want to create an environment that is perfect for all the microbes to get busy and rot your food scraps, yard waste, and any manure that you've added, until that mixture has been transformed into a perfect soil additive.

If you have seen an active compost pile that looks like nothing more than a heap of rotting food scraps and lawn cuttings, you know it still has a way to go until it is ready to be used in your garden. By ensuring that you provide enough moisture and ventilation, you only must wait, and that pile of rotting food and grass will eventually become a dirt like substance that can be mixed into your garden.

For a successful compost, turn it every couple of weeks. This helps aerate the material and evenly distribute the microbes, so they can digest the organic matter quickly.

Composts can be nothing more than a pile in the far corner of your yard, a series of commercial barrels that can be rotated so you do not need to mix the contents yourself, or you can simply use a large plastic tub. Regardless of where you put your compost, it is a good idea to keep the surrounding area clean and neat to try and deter pests and small animals that may want to dig and feast on your compost.

Regardless of the type of container or pile you use; it should be filled only to the halfway mark before you start another compost container or pile. Over-filling will reduce the air flow and available moisture for the microbes and slow down the processing.

Now that you understand the process, we can look at the actual structure and how you fill it with food scraps, manure, and dry organic waste. An ideal compost bin will have sides that are able to not only hold in the compost but at the same time allow moisture and air to pass through. If you are looking at a commercial product, make sure that there are sufficient ventilation holes in the sides and top to allow air flow throughout the entire structure.

If you are building your own compost bin or container, try to incorporate either slats or mesh as part of the structure to allow for air flow. The choice of materials is left up to your skill, budget, and personal aesthetics other than the caveat to avoid all forms of pressure treated lumber. The preservatives in this material can poison and potentially kill any microbes in contact with pressure treated wood products.

Once you have your container selected, you can start to fill it. The bottom layer needs to be an inch or so of dry organic material, such as shredded paper, fallen leaves, or cardboard. On top of this add wet organics, such as manure, lawn clippings or pruning, and food scraps. Once you have an inch or so of wet organic material, you need to cover that with a layer of dry organics. This pattern is repeated until you have filled up your container. As we already covered, you need to keep stirring it up and let it compost until it resembles a moist black dirt. It is only then that you can add it to your garden.

Once your compost is ready for use, you will need to decide how to apply it. There are two schools of thought as to how to do this. But for now, you simply need to decide if you are going to remove all the remains of the harvested plants and dig up your soil in the fall after the harvest. You would then work the compost into the disturbed soil and leave it to rest during the winter, in preparation for spring planting.

The other option is that you only pull out the plant stalks in the fall and leave the soil unworked. You would then top-dress the garden bed in the spring before you plant your seeds or transplant in your seedlings.

Regardless of which approach you prefer, you will have added the nutrients and minerals from your compost into your soil, and your next summer's plants will benefit.

# Chapter 10: Fertilizers

*"Fertilizer does no good in a heap, but a little spread around works miracles all over."*
— Richard Brinsley Sheridan

10-10-10, 15-1-12, 8-19-2. These numbers appear in my dreams when the spring is almost here. What do they mean? Well, it took me quite some time to figure them all out, so I am going to give you a crash course, so you know what you are looking at when you are at your local garden supply store.

## What do all the numbers mean?

All those numbers you see on the bags of fertilizer do in fact have a meaning and are not just poor attempts at branding. When taken together, these numbers are known as the fertilizer grade. The meaning of the numbers and what they mean is part of a national standard.

So enough of the preamble. In simple terms the numbers represent the percentage of the three primary fertilizer components in the bag. The first number is the level of Nitrogen (N), the second is Phosphorus (P), and then third is Potassium (K).

If you see a bag labeled 10-10-10, you know that the bag contains ten percent of all three of the primary components. If the bag is marked 15-1-12, that means that the fertilizer is fifteen percent N, one percent P, and twelve percent K. The remainder of the material in the bag will be some form of inert filler that may help aerate your soil.

That seems clear. But if we think about it a bit more, you are going to ask, how do I know what I need? It's great to be able to read the bags but that doesn't tell me how much of which I need in my soil.

## Proper levels

The common application is to one pound of N, P, and K per one hundred feet of growing rows. Yeah, I can hear you loud and clear. What does that mean in relation to a bag of fertilizer?

To figure out how much N, P, and K is in a bag of fertilizer, you need to know the weight of the bag, which will be printed on it. Saying it is heavy is not quite specific enough in this case. Once you find the weight, you need to note the three numbers.

If we use 10-10-10 as an example, mostly because the math is easy, then we will already know there is ten percent of N, P, and K in this bag. If the bag is fifty pounds, we know there are five pounds each of N, P, and K in that bag.

The next calculation is to determine the area of your garden beds. This can be figured out by the number of beds times the length of each one. Once you have that number, you will know how far that single bag of 10-10-10 will have to be spread and if you will need more than one.

Fine. But why are there different fertilizers with different numbers and how would I use them?

To explain this, we are going to need some more math so you might need to refill your drink or grab a snack first. We will continue once you are settled in again.

Right. The amount of fertilizer you need to apply is based on the current N, P, and K levels of your soil. Remember that soil test you skipped, well it might be worth shopping around to see if you can find one that will give you the N, P, K levels in your soil.

Obviously, you can still garden without knowing these numbers, but it will take many years of slow soil modification to get the N, P, and K levels where they need to be. The difficulty you will face is that the consequences of adding too much to the soil can be significant and the excess N, P, and K cannot be easily removed from the soil without digging it all up and starting again.

If there is too much Nitrogen in the soil, most of the plants will have incredible leaf and stalk growth with no fruit production. While this might be ideal for a leafy green crop, such as lettuce or spinach, it is not what you want for tomatoes or squash plants.

An excess of Phosphorus will have a similar effect of too high a soil pH and will effectively kill the plants in the affected soil. Likewise, if you add too much Potassium, it will reduce the plant's ability to absorb nutrients from the soil, starving the plants and possibly killing them.

So, let's get back to that soil test. The following tables summarize how much extra N, P, and K that you need to add to your soil to raise it to the optimum level for your vegetable garden.

**Pounds of Nitrogen to add per 100 square feet of soil.**

| Existing Soil Nitrogen Level PPM | Organic Matter (0 to 1%) | Organic Matter (1.1 to 2.0%) | Organic Matter (> 2.1%) |
|---|---|---|---|
| 0 - 9 | 0.55 | 0.44 | 0.33 |
| 10-19 | 0.44 | 0.33 | 0.21 |
| 20-29 | 0.33 | 0.21 | 0.1 |
| 30-39 | 0.21 | 0.1 | 0 |
| 40-49 | 0.1 | 0 | 0 |
| 50 - >50 | 0 | 0 | 0 |

**Pounds of Phosphorous to add per 100 square feet of soil.**

| Existing Soil Phosphorus PPM | Phosphorus to add |
|---|---|
| 0 - 3 | 5 |
| 4 - 7 | 4 |
| 8 - 11 | 3 |
| 12 - 14 | 1 |
| > 14 | 0 |

**Pounds of Potassium to add per 100 square feet of soil.**

| Existing Soil Potassium PPM | Potassium to add |
|---|---|
| 0 - 60 | 3 |
| 61 - 120 | 2 |
| 121 - 180 | 1 |
| > 181 | 0 |

Armed with all these numbers, you can now figure out how much Nitrogen, Phosphorus, and Potassium you need to apply to your soil to bring it into the ideal range for your plants. Once you have done the math you might be surprised to find that one of the bags of fertilizer at your garden center is pretty much on the mark with the correct numbers. But before you get too excited remember it is better that your fertilizer numbers be a little low than high.

Now that you know how to figure out what type and how much fertilizer to apply to your garden. Ah, but before we leave this behind, I know that some of you are wondering about your compost.

As I mentioned in that section, your compost is basically taking the nutrients from the scrap food and yard waste and making them available to the plants in your garden. In a perfect world you would also test your compost to determine its N, P, and K levels to make sure you are adding the proper amount.

In real life the actual levels of these nutrients in most composts are so low that even if your soil is at the perfect levels for all of them already, the addition of your compost will have only a minor impact overall.

This does not apply if you are bringing in truckloads of commercial compost and are planning to mix that in with your soil. In this case it would be beneficial to have your soil and the compost tested to make sure they will produce a good growing soil when mixed. A simple soil test may save you a great deal of money and time if you find out that your soil is already good or that adding the extra compost will add too much of any of the three critical nutrients.

## Types

As with almost everything in our modern lives, garden fertilizers are available in several varieties. You are likely to see brand labels that proudly proclaim their product is organic, inorganic, slow release, controlled release, dry, and wet. Sounds a tad confusing to me, so we are going to look at each claim to understand what it really means and how that will affect your choice.

### *Organic*
These are fertilizers that have been sourced from plants and animals.

A note about the term, organic. In this instance, the first definition of the word is being used, namely that the material in question is related to or derived from living matter. The second, and currently more popular definition, is that the material is produced without the use of chemicals or other artificial agents. This may or may not be applicable, depending on the supplier of the organic fertilizer.

## *Inorganic*

These are fertilizers that are either mined or synthesized from chemicals. What this means in practice is that you are most likely looking at either a pellet or liquid form of fertilizer.

## *Dry*

When you are in your garden supply store looking to get some fertilizer, you will see that in addition to the organic and inorganic division there are both wet and dry products on the shelf.

Dry fertilizers are typically intended to either broadcast spread as they are. The recommended amount per one hundred square feet will be on the packaging. These products are usually designed for lawns, and as such, the application instructions may seem confusing.

However, if you did the math and figured out the application schedule for your garden, these fertilizers can be extremely effective.

## *Wet*

You will also see on the shelves a great number of bottles of fertilizers. These are, in effect, the dry material that has then been hydrated to make it simpler to use. If you do not want the hassle of doing the math on the dry products, these will be ideal for you.

As with all the other types of fertilizers, application rates should be on the packaging. Another note about organic and inorganic fertilizers is needed here: When you plan all the options for fertilizer for your garden, remember that if you are looking to use only organic products, in the popular and second definition meaning, then you will be limited to sourcing an organic certified manure that comes from animals or plants that are certified as organic or have been fed certified feed.

Any of the liquid fertilizers will be from inorganic sources, as this is the only way to economically verify the N, P, and K values of the product for mass production. It is also safe to assume that all dry fertilizers are also from an inorganic source unless it is clearly stated on the label. The one trick that I have run into is for a dry fertilizer supplier to state that the product is organic, but they use the first definition of the word, derived from living matter. As the consumer, make sure you understand the product that you are purchasing.

## *Slow and Time Release*

The final type of fertilizer you will encounter during your travels are the ones marked "slow release" and "timed". This is achieved either by coating the fertilizer in a material that dissolves slowly and releases the fertilizer to the soil a bit at a time, or the fertilizer itself has been modified for slow dissolving and will take some time to fully incorporate into the soil.

Most times when you need fertilizer, it is considered a good practice to use a combination of slow and quick release products. This will help your plants establish rapidly and still provide the longer-term nutrients they need.

Finding and using the correct fertilizer requires a little bit of effort on your part but the rewards of the fall bounty are worth it.

# Chapter 12: Water

*"If there is magic on this planet, it is contained in water."*

— Loren Eiseley

We all know that without water there is no life, but did you know that there are different types of water? And that each type of water will affect your plants differently? Some of you are nodding your heads in understanding, but for the rest of us that did not grow up in a greenhouse, let me explain.

## Types of Water

When you think of water, I am going to guess the first image that comes to mind is the tap water in your house. This is quickly followed by rain, rivers, lakes, the ocean, and perhaps snow or water wells.

We all have a pretty good grasp on the different sources of water, but not many people understand how the source impacts the quality of that water.

## Source Impact

So, why does it matter where your water comes from? To understand how important your water source is, you need look no further than your kitchen. To make a pot of coffee, you add your grounds to water. In a few minutes you have that all important morning brew.

Now, instead of making it from regular water, try to imagine how it would taste if it was made with sparkling water, or perhaps apple juice, or even milk? These are all variations of water that are perfect in the correct environment, but not so good for coffee.

If you use a residential water supply, fluoride and pH stabilizers may have been added for health and to keep the distribution pipes from rusting. The presence of fluoride will have no effect on your plants, but the pH stabilizer will.

If you are watering with pH stabilized city water, it will normally have been adjusted to a pH of 7.

This seems fine on the surface, but if you are growing basil, which has a preferred pH range of between six and seven-and-a-half, alongside some parsley, which likes a soil pH of between five-and-a-half and six-and-a-half, when you water you increase the pH too high.

The higher pH will not kill your herbs, but you will notice they are not as productive as plants that are watered with rainwater that has a typical pH of six. Not surprisingly, most of the plants that we grow in our gardens are well-adapted to growing in rainwater.

In addition to the pH of your water supply you also need to be aware of other contents that may be harmful to either your plants or to you. We will look at the most common water supplies that are used for watering vegetable gardens, the hazards associated with each one, and what the solutions are to make sure that both you and your plants are happy and healthy.

### *City Water*

If you live in an urban location, you will have access to your local municipal or city water supplies. This water is often sourced from lakes and rivers, man-made reservoirs, or deep wells that tap into an aquifer below the surface.

All this water is treated when it is pumped from the source and before it is delivered to your house. The treatments often include the addition of fluoride, a pH buffer to neutralize the water, and chlorine to kill any harmful bacteria that may be present in the water or any section of the piping that leads to your house.

For those of us who have been living in the city, we will soon become accustomed to taste or smell the chlorine that is added to the water unless there is some contamination event like a storm that may have affected the water supply.

One of the difficulties of using city water is the impact on your plants will be slow and hard to notice if you do not have any plants that are on a different water supply. As far as you can tell, all your plants will be growing well and look healthy as they are able to somewhat adapt to the less-than-ideal conditions.

If you have noticeable chlorine levels in your water, fill a container with water and let it sit in an open container for a couple days. This will give enough time for all the chlorine to off-gas out of the water. This will not change the pH, but there will no longer be any chlorine to burn your plants.

A far more significant hazard associated with your tap water is the presence of lead. If we use New York city as an example, we will see that over 40 percent of all the buildings in the city have lead pipes either in the buildings or are using lead service pipes to connect the building to the city water mains under the streets.

The health problems associated with elevated lead levels in your tap water include anemia, nerve disorders, kidney damage, headaches, and memory loss to name just a few common symptoms.

If you have lead in your water and you use your tap water for your garden, the lead in the water will be absorbed by the plants. The lead will concentrate in any root vegetables, such as carrots and potatoes, and render them unfit to eat.

As you may guess, it is critical to get your residential water tested. This is not only for the health of your garden plants, but for the health of you and your family.

## *Rainwater*

### Nature

The simplest approach is to make sure there are no trees or buildings that will shelter your garden, and let nature do the watering for you. This might work, and it might not. We've all heard about drought issues that are affecting the commercial farms. So, unless you live in a wet area, such as the Pacific Northwest, where there is usually enough rain to look after your garden, you will need to augment the rain.

Unless you happen to live in Colorado, you are allowed to collect at least some rainwater to help look after your garden. Given the potential difficulties in using city water, you might think that rainwater is the perfect solution.

You are mostly correct in terms of the quality of the water. Difficulties arise from trying to find large enough surfaces to collect the water from. There is the additional obstacle of storing the water until you need it, as the rain that you have collected will have also watered your garden at the same time.

If you happen to live in an urban house, you may be able to use your roof as a catchment surface and the gutters and downspouts to direct this water into some form of water storage container. On the other hand, if you live in a rental or an apartment, you may not have either access to collect rainwater, nor any location suitable for storing it.

We are not going to go into all the details around rain catchment beyond a couple fifty-gallon tubs under your downspouts.

Once you have your fifty-gallon drums under your downspouts, there is little left to do other than cover them with a fine mesh so the standing water will not become a breeding ground for mosquitoes and other nuisance insects.

Most rainwater will have a pH of about 6, which is perfect for most plants that you may want to grow. There may be microscopic traces of pollutants in the water depending on your local air quality, but this is only noticeable in lab tests and should have no detrimental effects on you or your plants.

If it is possible to only use rainwater for your garden, your plants will be much happier and productive, but if you only have access to tap water, you can still grow a very productive garden.

## Delivering Water

Unlike your soil, there is very little you can do to modify your water that makes any sort of financial sense. Obviously, there are reverse osmosis filters that can make any type of water clean and safe to drink but these are complex and expensive pieces of technology. Unless your water test reveals a potentially harmful contamination, such as lead, you can use the water that you have access to grow your garden.

# Irrigation

Understanding the differences between the most common sources of water for your garden is only the first step towards happy and healthy plants. The next thing to consider is how to get all that water to your plants where and when they need it.

You can readily test to see if you are giving your plant enough water by pushing your finger into the soil a couple inches. If the soil is dry, you need to add more water. If the soil is damp, you are watering the correct amount. If the soil is wet and waterlogged, you need to water less.

## *Watering Can*

The most important thing to remember when you are thinking about watering your plants is that water is heavy. Heavier than you would really like it to be.

We have all likely seen those nostalgic images of the old-fashioned watering can and the huge garden. I am not going to say that watering cans do not have a place in a modern urban garden, because they do, but unless you are built of stronger stuff than I am, I don't think you want to do all your watering with one.

We mentioned the watering can as a heavy and potentially difficult option, but it might be the perfect solution if you only need to additionally water your plants every now and then.

What should you look for in a watering can? I can give the annoying but accurate answer, "That depends." I know it is a cop out so I am going to explain what features you should look for.

Do we want to start with form or function? Some people love the looks of a certain item and are willing to work around functional issues. If you are in this camp, really, I have very little to add that will help, other than to make sure it holds water. The specifics of how easy it is to fill, the length of the neck, and the watering head will be determined by the style and design.

The flip side of this is to choose function over form. If you are more concerned that your watering can is up to the job, there are a few guidelines that I can suggest.

The first thing to look at is whether the handle fits your hand. Is it comfortable? Smooth and easy to hold onto? Once you have found a watering can that passes that test, you can go to the next step.

How much does it hold? And regardless always of what you may have heard, bigger is not better. Ideally, your choice of watering should hold about a gallon of water when it is full. The trick to remember is that you don't have to fill it up to use it. But that gallon of water will come in handy as you near the fall harvest and your plants need extra water to ripen their produce.

The final thing to consider is the neck and the watering head style. Ideally, the watering head will be the shower type that allows a delicate rain-like deluge of water where you point it. If there is no watering head the water will come out in a solid stream. You will need to be more careful when you water with this design, so you do not wash away the soil or dig a hole.

Using a watering can will give you the time to look over each plant carefully. An important note if you are thinking of using a watering can is that your plants will need an ever-increasing amount of water as the growing season progresses.

To give you an idea of this increase, let's look at the water needs of a typical tomato plant. During germination it only requires that the soil be kept moist. Once it has been transplanted into your garden, it will need about two-thirds of a gallon a week as it starts to grow, and the roots get established.

Once the tomato plant starts to set fruit, it will be looking for an additional half gallon or more each week, depending on how hot and dry the summer is. As you near the fall harvest and your tomato plant is now festooned with lovely ripe fruit, it will easily use an extra gallon every week. Each plant is now looking for almost two and a half gallons of water each week.

As you can see, you will need to give each plant more water as the season progresses, which can be time and labor intensive if you use a watering can, but not out of the realm of possibility.

## *Garden Hose*

The most widely used method to water a garden is the lowly hose. If you are using your city water and have a hose bib that is close enough to reach, the hose will offer an unlimited supply of water. If you are watering with collected rainwater, you will need a pump to hook up your hose.

When you are buying a hose, or if you want to make sure that your existing ones are good enough, there are a couple simple little tests you can do. First, see if it is long enough to reach all your plants.

I am not talking about being able to spray the plant from across the yard but bring the hose to the plant. This matters because the closer the hose is to the plant has a direct effect on how that water is delivered to each plant.

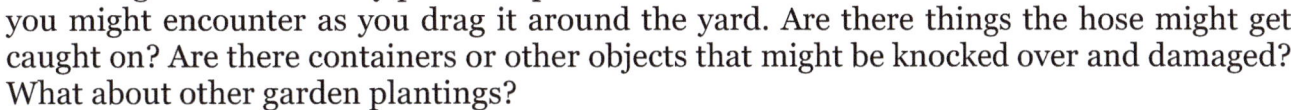

The best way to water your plants is using a high volume and low-pressure water flow. This will ensure there is sufficient water for the plants and that the pressure is low enough to not wash away the soil. To be able to water this way, you need to have the hose directly beside the plant in question.

Once you know that your hose is long enough, the next thing to look for is any potential problems that you might encounter as you drag it around the yard. Are there things the hose might get caught on? Are there containers or other objects that might be knocked over and damaged? What about other garden plantings?

The last thing that you want to do is either to damage things in your yard or drag the hose over the plants that you are so carefully looking after as you tend to them. Walk through the process you will follow to water your plants. You can have the water running if you want, but it is a bit easier if the water to the hose is off.

If you find items that might be knocked over, figure out if they can be moved or if you can avoid them by trying a different path or order of plant watering. The same applies to other garden beds. If you find areas that the hose wants to damage, then a simple fix is to hammer a piece of metal, such as rebar or some other inexpensive long skinny item into the ground to force the hose away from the item or plant in danger. For in-ground garden beds, if you put a stake or metal rod at each corner, these should protect your plants from hose-related damage.

Once you have the correct length of hose, you will need some type of flow control on the business end, so you don't waste water or drown your plants. The most common control is the pistol grip spray nozzle.

Now, these pistol grip sprayers are fantastic for washing your car; they are not that good at watering your plants. They increase the speed of the water being delivered and can potentially damage your plants or wash away the soil, you spent so much time perfecting.

If you can afford to get one of the long metal hose wands that has the shower head attachment, these are ideal. Using the integrated shut off, you can control the flow and water pressure so you can deliver a high-volume, low-pressure water supply to your plants.

If you cannot afford a watering wand, turn down the water pressure at the hose bib or pump, and then kink the hose to stop the water flow as you change plants. This will eventually damage the hose, but I am talking about many years of abuse before you will need to replace the hose.

While using a hose to water your plants makes the job simple, the most common reason gardeners prefer to use a hose is that it takes longer than any sort of automated system. Yep, you heard me clearly. A hose is preferred because it takes longer to do the job. Now, this is not as crazy as it seems at first glance. Let me explain.

Why are you growing a garden? I know we started with this question but bear with me here. The experienced gardeners know where I am going, so I will ask you to keep quiet for just a bit longer. I would hate to spoil the surprise.

No matter why you started to grow your own food, it will not be very long before you discover you have become unknowingly infected, and watering with a hose is just the most visible symptom of your new affliction. Any ideas?

The outdoors.

Yep, even though you may have the most incredible home theater or gaming system ever seen, the simple pleasure of spending time outside in the sun will have a far more powerful attraction than technology.

Hence, the preference to use a garden hose for watering. You are looking after your investment, with the bonus that you no longer must justify spending time outside in the sun. Consider watering with a hose as fresh air and sunlight therapy that you can do whenever you feel the need and for as long as you want.

Now, not everyone has the time to hand water all the plants in the garden, even if they really want to. This is why there are other options to ensure all your plants are looked after.

## *Sprinklers*

I know that I included a picture of a sprinkler watering a garden at the beginning of the section, so you might be wondering why I am now going to tell you that using your sprinkler is a bad idea.

The thing to remember when it comes to watering your garden is there is a world of difference between what is ideal and what is available and at hand.

In a perfect setup, I would recommend against using a lawn sprinkler to water your garden because they are inaccurate and wastewater. The difficulty comes from their design. Watering a lawn is a different task than watering a garden, even though they are all plants.

Your lawn is a wide-open space that is covered in plants that love lots of water. Estimates vary, but when it rains, the first inch or two of water is absorbed by the lawn before any water makes it to the underlying soil.

Using a sprinkler to water your garden will water your plants, but a great deal of is being wasted.

If you have a garden bed with both tomatoes and lettuce growing in it, the lettuce may get enough water from the excess that the tomato plant can't use. But when you use a lawn sprinkler, you are giving all your plants the same amount of water and risk either drowning some plants or shortchanging the thirsty ones.

If you only have a lawn sprinkler, then use it. If this is the case, you will need to keep a close eye on your plants for signs of stress from over-or under-watering.

## *Drip Irrigation*

The next step up the ladder in watering your plants is to install an automated system. These take care of the scheduling and watering for you but do come at a cost both financially and in complexity.

A typical automated watering system starts with the pump to provide the water. If you are on city water, then a timer-controlled solenoid will turn the water "on" when needed and turn it "off" when the watering is done.

After the water control, there will be one or more filters. As the wet end of the system is either a soaker hose or micro drippers, the water flowing to them needs to be free of any debris that will plug them off and stop the flow of the water.

Following the filter is the distribution hose. This will lead to each garden bed, row, or container where your plants grow. At each plant there will be a micro dripper to supply drops of water to the soil beside individual plant stalks. These drippers can be calibrated between half a gallon an hour up to two gallons an hour or more. Working in conjunction with the pump or solenoid timer, you have excellent control of the amount of water that is delivered to each plant each day.

By incorporating several timers on the branch lines running off the main distribution hose, you can easily adjust the watering schedule for each garden bed, row, or container depending on how you configure the system. This will enable you to make sure that ripening tomatoes get enough to drink while not drowning the lettuce or spinach.

The other option is to hook up a soaker hose instead of the distribution hose. In this set up you simply route the soaker hose around all the plants that need the same amount of water.

While an automated system takes the day-to-day chore out of watering your plants, it does come with its own maintenance headaches. If your pump or water solenoid dies, then your plants go without. The same can be said for your timer. If it fails to work as expected, your plants will again go without. Finally, there is the filter. It will need to be replaced more often than you would like, and they are surprisingly expensive.

As there are continual improvements and advances in automated garden watering systems, I would recommend that you browse through your local hardware big box store, as more and more of what was once commercial irrigation equipment is now being sold to the public.

If you are thinking about an automated system, be prepared to spend some time checking the drippers and filters each time you are in the garden.

Regardless of how you ultimately decide to water your garden, part of that chore is spending time outside, hopefully in the sunshine, so it is enjoyable. Plus, you will see first-hand how well your garden is growing,

# Chapter 13: Germination

*"A seed neither fears light nor darkness, but uses both to grow."*

– Matshona Dhliwayo

To grow your garden, you need to start your plants. This can be either from seeds or from cuttings. The easiest and most cost-effective method is to grow your plants from seed. While this will save you a great deal of money, the tradeoff is extra time and effort.

When you were last at your local garden center, I am sure that you noticed the huge displays of seeds. If you spend any time looking through them, you will see there are seemingly endless types of plants and usually multiple varieties of popular plants, such as tomatoes.

So how do you know what to choose? Is one brand of Roma tomatoes better than another? What about all the types of lettuce? One brand has nine types of lettuce while you can find on-line vendors that will happily sell you any one of hundreds of different types.

When you are getting your seeds together for your first garden, I would recommend you ask your local garden supply store which seeds will work best in your local climate. With a year or two of gardening under your belt, you will have a good idea of what you like to grow, and which brands grow best. Once you have a grasp on how to garden, the entire world of seeds is at your fingertips.

Now that you have your handful of seeds all ready to go the next step will be to get them started.

## Seeds

1. The most common and easiest test to see if your seeds will grow is to plant them.
    a. Now this is supposed to be a viability test, so don't get carried away and plant all your seeds. To do a test planting you will need a small container that can hold a couple inches of soil. Make sure the soil is damp and follow the directions in the appropriate growing guide for the seeding depth, suggested temperature and if the seed needs darkness or light.
    b. Prepare your seeds as required and put the container on a bright windowsill and wait. Usually in a week or two you will start to see small seedlings pushing through the soil.
    c. Count the number of seedlings that have sprouted and compare that to the number of seeds you planted. You did record that, right? If you have more than 75 percent of the seeds growing, that should be good enough to justify planting the rest of the seeds.
    d. If you find that half or fewer of the seeds germinate, you should look for a different seed source, as these seeds are no longer considered viable.

2. The next way to test the viability of your seeds is to put them in a bowl or glass of water. If the seeds are good, they will sink to the bottom of the water while the non-viable seeds will float on the surface.
    a. A significant drawback to this technique is that your seeds are wet. The moisture will have started the germination process and these seeds will now need to be planted.
    b. If you are going to test your seeds this way, do it the same day as you are planning to put the seeds in the soil.
3. The final way to determine seed viability is to look at them.
    a. Obviously, this will only be of any use if you know what you are looking at and what a non-viable seed looks like. Once you have gardened for a few years you will develop a good eye when you look at seeds, and then this technique will come into its own.

With your tested seeds, or shiny new store-bought seeds in hand you can now get started on getting the seeds started.

If you look at the back of seed packages you will see some details on how to get your seeds started. The basics requirements to get a seed to germinate and start growing is some dirt, water, and usually darkness from being buried in soil at some depth.

With that theory in hand, the specifics to make your seeds burst into life are as follows. Find a flat tray that can hold soil that is at least twice the depth as what is required on the seed packs. Make sure that the soil is moist, but not saturated with water.

Using either a pen, pencil, or your fingertip make a series of indents in the soil to the depth specified on the seed packs. These holes can be a half inch or less apart as the plants will be transplanted before they get large enough to be a problem to each other.

The next step is to put two seeds into each indent. With two seeds in each space, there is a better chance there will be a seedling to transplant. Finally cover the indent with a thin layer of soil

## *Germination*

With your seeds covered in a lightly tamped layer of damp soil, all you need to do now is wait. A good suggestion is to put an event in the calendar in your phone for when the seeds are most likely to have germinated. Information on germination times can be found in the growing guide chapter of this book or on the back of the seed package.

It is important that you keep the soil moist for the duration of that germination time. If you are so inclined, you can mist the soil every couple days to make sure that it doesn't dry out.

An easier approach is to put the container full of soil in a clear plastic bag. You need to make sure the plastic bag is well-sealed to keep all the moisture inside. Once the first set of leaves have emerged from the soil, you need to remove the plastic bag.

These first set of leaves are known as cotyledons. Also called seed leaves, these are part of the seed themselves and provide energy to the growing plant to allow it to access the stored energy in the seed and start growing.

Cotyledons will last until the plant has produced enough true leaves to sustain it. If you happen to have a plant identification book at hand and are trying to identify your new seedling based on these first leaves, you will have a very difficult time. Cotyledons are all very similar in appearance and may or may not have any characteristics or appearance in common with the full-grown plant.

It is true leaves that will eventually develop the characteristic features of the full-grown plant. When the true leaves start to appear in the week or two following the cotyledons, you need to put the seedlings in the correct light level preferred by the full-grown plants. If you leave your seedlings in a darker area than they are looking for, they will start to elongate and stretch out, get leggy.

While you might have a thing for long thin legs, legginess in your seedlings is not desirable. If you come across leggy seedlings, think of them as the runts of the litter, and as such, they will need special care and attention for their entire lives.

# Seedlings

The other approach to starting your plants is to buy already established seedlings. You will not have to bother testing the seeds, making sure they germinate, and keeping them alive until their true leaves are established.

By purchasing existing seedlings, you are also going to be planting the most viable plants, as the weaker and potentially leggy plants will have been already culled by the garden staff. The trade-off for getting pre-grown seedlings is the price. While the cost of a package of seeds varies, you can expect to pay about the same price for a single happy seedling from your greenhouse that is ready to start life in your garden as you would pay for an entire package of seeds.

## *Availability*

In addition to the cost of the seedlings, you are also limited to the varieties of plants that the garden supply store has in stock. This is both good and bad. Let me explain: When you are learning about gardening, it can be helpful to have seedlings that you know will grow and do well in your local area.

You can be sure that the seedlings at your local garden center will thrive in your area.

Once you gain more experience and knowledge about growing your own food, you will know if the varieties sold locally are the ones that you still want to grow, or if you want to experiment with more exotic varieties that may not be in high demand.

For most people gardening is the beginning of a lifelong addiction, where you can fine tune the type and variety of vegetables that you grow. Remember those purple carrots, black tomatoes, and rainbow-colored corn we mentioned earlier? Unless you happen to live near an incredible garden nursery, you will not find any of these as seedlings.

I recommend that for the first year or two of gardening that you try a combination of seeds that you germinate and seedlings from the nursery. This is the "belt and suspenders" approach. If your seeds don't germinate for some reason, you still have happy viable plants for your garden. If your seeds do germinate, you will have a garden full of amazing produce.

I know of many seasoned gardeners who continue to plant a mix of self-germinated seeds and nursery seedlings even after decades of experience. This approach allows you to focus on the new and interesting seeds that you want to try each year while still knowing that you have strong reliable plants for your core harvested crops.

The final benefit of using a nursery seedling over your own is timing. Unless you are willing to invest the time in the late part of the winter to start your seeds, make sure they germinate, have had plenty of time to develop their true leaves, and are strong enough to transplant outside, you will be missing valuable growing time.

## *Be safe.*

While all these benefits will make nursery and garden supply store seedlings very appealing, you need to exercise some caution. I know, it seems that everything in life requires caution these days, but the precautions around buying seedlings are simple.

When you are standing in front of that display of what looks like thousands of small tomato plants, or herbs, or pumpkins you need to take a deep breath and pause for a moment. It is fine that the crowd is pushing you aside in their haste to grab some plants. Let them panic and soon you will be alone with the plants, and you can begin your search for the best ones.

To start with, you should ignore any plants that have wilted leaves, especially if the soil is either rock hard and dry or soaking wet and dripping mud. These are not happy and healthy plants. If they survive being transplanted into your garden, it is unlikely they will be great producers over the summer and into harvest.

You might be surprised to see that these stressed plants have been placed strategically near the front, so they are the first to be grabbed. Finding a strong happy plant will require a bit more effort on your part.

Most seedlings will have been grown in plastic containers divided into several sections. Typically, a couple seeds will have been put into each section to make sure that at least one plant germinates in each. You are looking for strong plants, and by that, I mean each plant is a good solid shade of green, not the washed-out light green of a key lime pie. These pasty plants should also be left for the panic buyers in the next customer wave after lunch.

Once you have spotted the seedlings that are a rich green, it is time to examine their leaves. Are they fully spread out or curled in at the edges? If they are curled, the plant is or has been stressed and should be left for someone less knowledgeable.

Now that you have spotted a seedling with firm, non-drooping leaves that are spread wide, eagerly searching for the sun, give it a delicate tug. No, don't rip it out of the soil, just a gentle tug.

If the stalk moves, you need to move on. This is an indication of minimal root development, and the plant will suffer a greater transplant shock when you put it in your garden compared to a seedling with a more developed root structure.

Remember, all the seedlings cost the same, regardless of their health, so it is worth taking a few minutes to make sure you get the best plants for your money. Not only will these plants be healthier and happier during the summer, but they will also be more resistant to pests and will usually produce a better harvest.

The final thing you need to be looking out for while you search for ideal seedlings is the presence of pests. Chewed leaves and possibly even seeing an aphid or spider mite is a good indication that you should just stop and grab a coffee at your local coffee joint. Once aphids and spider mites get established, they are annoyingly difficult to eliminate.

Once you have your pest-free and happy seedlings in hand you are pretty much ready to start gardening.

## Care

Now that you have either your seeds growing, your seedlings happily hanging out, or your cuttings all ready and anxious to get producing, you need to look after them until they are ready to be moved outside into your garden.

As with your established plants, the seedlings, and cuttings you are now responsible for need a combination of light, water, and heat for them to thrive. The important thing to know about all your young charges is that they are very sensitive. That extra couple hours in the sunshine that an adult plant will happily accept can be enough to kill a seedling or newly established cutting. The same applies to watering and heat.

### *Light*

Everything needs some light to live. So once the true leaves have emerged on your seedlings or your cuttings have recovered from their transplant shock, you need to make sure you are giving them enough light to thrive.

How do you know how much is enough? We've already discussed light and all its complexity, but the reality, even when they are young delicate seedlings, is the light from a bright south facing window will be more than enough to keep your seedlings happy and thriving.

But that window is in my living room, and I don't have any space behind the couch so what do I do? Or in the kitchen, or even worse, your house is north-facing, and you have no southern sunny windows. On the surface this might sound like a problem, but you'll be surprised by how simple the solution is. All you need is a bright light.

So, let's start with the type of light. You're looking for a basic grow light, as the needs of the seedlings are simple. I'm not suggesting that you head out and buy a fancy high-tech grow light suited for some illegal grow-op or hydroponics greenhouse. Nope, I am talking about the standard replacement grow light bulb that is now on the market, or even the simple LED bar lights that are designed as grow lights.

When you set up your lights, you want to make sure that your seedlings are getting enough light. As we mentioned, what we see for light is not always what your plants see. The solution for this is to put your new light bulb or LED light bar about a foot above your seedlings. As the plants grow, keep an eye on their leaves. If they start to look bleached or curled up and crispy, you need to raise the lights a couple inches.

If you are starting a small tray of seedlings, you can use something as simple as that old adjustable arm light that you used on your desk as a kid, or maybe your friend has one that's no longer needed. Set the light so that your new grow-light bulb shines evenly over your seedlings. If it is possible to have the light bulb centered over top of the tray, they will grow straight towards the light, and in time, be ideal for transplanting.

If you cannot put the light above your seedlings but must light from the side, you will need to rotate your seedlings every few days to keep them growing straight. You'll be surprised how fast your seedlings will lean and grow towards the light if you forget to rotate them, your seedlings can still be transplanted outside once they are ready and the weather is warm enough, even if they are leaning over like someone at Mardi Gras. But they may need a few extra days to get established in their new home.

When you get your light set up and working, make sure your seedlings get a period of dark each day. Depending on your routines, it might be enough for you to simply turn off the light each evening and turn it back on in the morning. But if your day is anywhere near as chaotic as mine, it will be much easier to plug your grow light into a timer. Ideally, your seedlings will get twelve to fourteen hours of light each day, followed by a period of dark. These are perfect conditions, so the closer you can get to achieving this, the happier your plants will be.

## Water

With your seedlings happily growing either in a bright windowsill or under a grow light, your main chore is to keep them watered. Seedlings are not very thirsty, so you will need little more than a spray bottle to keep them hydrated and happy.

Every couple of days, check the moisture level in the soil. If the top of the soil is cracked or crumbles when you touch it, you need to spray it down. Just mist the soil and let the water absorb. Then mist it again until the moisture does not absorb immediately into the soil. You have added enough water, and the top surface remains shiny and moist for a while.

Unlike a larger plant, your seedlings are extremely susceptible to drowning if you add too much water at one time. You might be getting the idea that your seedlings are a great deal of work to keep alive. They do need some careful attention, but the good news is that they will quite rapidly outgrow your small seed starting setup and will be ready for transplanting. Once they are in their new homes, your seedlings will require quite a bit less work.

## Heat

Most of the plants we like to grow either for food or decoration are happiest when they are warm. Your seedlings are no exception to this. They will be much happier if they are kept warm around the clock. If you live somewhere warm, or keep your house heated like the tropics, your plants will not be able to understand their luck. If you happen to live in a cooler area or keep your place at a more reasonable temperature, you might need to invest in a heating mat.

These mats will help keep your seedlings from getting cold feet and encourage them to grow as tall and vigorously as they can. If you do not want to splurge for a heating mat, you could place your seedlings on top of a radiator if you have one, or over top a heating vent. The drawback of these techniques is the soil will dry out much faster and you will need to be much more vigilant on keeping the soil moist.

## Fertilizer

As we have already touched on fertilizer and using it in your soil you may think it would be helpful to add to either the soil or the water at this time. I can understand you wanting to encourage your plants as this is a very exciting time, but you would be wrong.

The simple answer is don't.

# Chapter 14: Transplanting

*"When you plant something, you invest in a beautiful future amidst a stressful, chaotic and, at times, downright appalling world."*

- Monty Don

The next critical skill you need to learn on your gardening journey is how to transplant a seedling. You are looking to move your delicate plants from the comfort they have known into the harsh wild outdoors of your garden. Ok, I hear you saying that you can only grow on your balcony and have started your seeds in their final pots, and you don't need to learn how to do this.

I suggest that learning how to transplant seedlings is in fact a skill worth learning. Why, do you ask? Because transplanting your seedlings is the same skill you use to keep any decorative houseplants alive, as well as any edible plants you might want to keep alive over the winter for example, ever-producing lettuce or indeterminate tomatoes.

So, there you sit, either keen to learn how to transplant or resigned to adding yet one more possibly redundant skill to your repertoire. I will try to make this interesting and concise to not bore you.

A common reason to transplant your plants is to take them from their crowded kindergarten classes and out into the real world of pests and competition found in your garden. It is only once your plants are in their new homes that they can grow to their potential.

# When Are They Ready to Move

So, when do you dig up your seedlings and subject them to such harsh treatment?

## *Outdoor Temp*

So, how do you know when it is warm enough outside? Well, that depends. I know that feels like a dodge. In this case I do know the answer and it does depend. It depends on the type of plant in question.

Broccoli and Kale can manage a light frost without any bad effects, but if you had transplanted a tomato or bell pepper, these would now be dead. It will take a couple days for the damage to be visible but there is no going back. You will need to replace these plants.

The common practice is to wait until after the last frost as we mentioned or to wait until the end of May. While this might be months late if you live in the south, the end of May might be too early some years if you are gardening in the north.

## *Soil Temp*

Not only does the air temperature need to be in the correct range for the plants you want to move, but the soil temperature does also as well. There is no benefit to rushing out your plants during one of those heat spells in the spring when the soil is still cold and potentially frozen some distance down.

As difficult as it may be, this is a time for patience. If you rush your plants, you run a good chance of killing them. Now, there are going to be years where the weather is all mixed up and a cold snap comes to visit after you have already transplanted all your plants.

If the weather forecasts this might happen, there are a couple maneuvers you can take to try to minimize the damage.

Firstly, if you are growing your plants in moveable pots or containers, bring them inside for the cold snap. While they will not have the light they are expecting, the effect of a few darker days will be far less than what the cold might do.

If you are growing in a raised-bed garden or in the soil, then obviously, you will not be able to bring all your plants back inside. And no, don't even think about it. It's far more damaging to your plants to dig them up and in effect transplant them into pots for a few days so they can avoid the cold.

If you are dealing with unmovable plants, you have three options. The easiest one is to ignore it. *Que sera sera.* Grab your favorite beverage, a good program to binge watch, and put the garden out of your head. Odds are quite good that if you are in a densely built-up area that the local temperature will not fall enough to kill your plants. You are likely to find some frost-burned leaves that will turn black and fall off in the coming days, but there is a good chance that your plants will only be set back a week or so before they get growing again.

The other two options depend on what you have around the house, and how concerned you are about what your neighbors think.

If you have a fan, the first option is to take a leaf from the frost-control strategies used by commercial outdoor growers. If you keep the air moving over your plants, the frost cannot settle and damage the fragile leaves. In a commercial setting, this is done with massive engine driven fans mounted on posts above the crop. Obviously, this is not possible in your garden, but if you have a floor fan, or a desk fan, or even one of those big workshop fans, you are in luck.

Drag that fan out and set it running. Now, not so fast that you blow the leaves off your plants but fast enough that there is some leaf movement. If possible, try to cover the entire garden with the fan. I am confident that you will find the best arrangement you can give your garden space and fan selection.

Once the fan is running, you can catch up on your binge TV watching and wait for the cold to leave before you turn the fans off and see if there has been any damage.

The final option is to gather all those extra quilts, duvets, and blankets that seem to fill up your closets without you ever seeing them arrive. Before it gets dark – mostly because it is crap to have to work outside in the cold and dark– drag all your blankets out to your garden.

Now, blankets are heavy, so you are going to need to make some type of framework strong enough to support blankets over top of your plants.

This will help keep your plants warm in the cold air, as the heat from the soil will be trapped by the blankets. Once you have put all your plants to bed, you can also head inside for your favorite beverage and catch up on the show.

The drawback to using your blankets is you will need to head outside bright and early each morning to uncover your garden. Now, if life gets in the way, try to leave the blankets in place no more than a day or two at the most. Any longer than that and you begin to starve the plants of light. And we know that plants without light are compost in waiting.

# Big Picture

Before you get your hands dirty, there are a couple terms that need explaining. When you talk to any gardener about transplanting and spring work you will hear mentioned "hardening off" and "transplant shock."

So, what do these terms mean?

# Hardening Off

Let's start with hardening off. The simple meaning is getting your plants used to a change in temperature and the reality of living outside. If you think about it for a moment, you will see what a transition you are putting your plants through.

So far, they have only ever had the constant conditions of your home. If you are like most people, you will keep your place comfortable and heated or cooled to somewhere around 23 degrees Celsius, or 70 degrees Fahrenheit. And not very surprisingly, this temperature is as relaxing and enjoyable for your plants as it is for you.

Do you enjoy camping? If you do, then you know that most nights are cooler than the day, and after a winter of staying inside your house, those first few nights spent in your tent will be chilly, even with your great sleeping bag. What about your first visit to the beach each summer? I am guessing there is a great deal of sunscreen applied, as well as some wide brimmed hats involved. That first exposure to the sun after a season spent indoors can be quite a shock, and even if you are well-prepared, you may end up with some spectacularly sunburned bits.

Well, your plants experience the same reaction to the sunlight, the cold, and even the wind. So, to ease their adjustment we put them through a process known as "hardening off." This adds a step between your plants growing in their germination container and their final spot in the garden.

# Best Practices to Ensure Survival

So, what do you do to give your plants the best chance to get established in your garden without too many stresses or problems? Well, you start by hardening them off.

Your seedlings will have been happily growing in some type of container or plastic flat for all their lives so far. The first step to moving them outside is to briefly expose them to their new environment and bring them back to the comfort of your home. The entire process can usually be done over a single week, though if the weather does not cooperate, you might need a few more days.

Once the daytime temperatures are in the range that your plants prefer, then all you need to do is to move their entire tray or pot that they are currently growing in, outside. Now don't go crazy and put them in the full sunlight but find a shaded but warm area that is out of any wind.

Let your plants relax outside for the day but bring them back inside before the temperature falls, and for sure before the sun sets. Put the flat or pot back inside and let your plants enjoy the warmth of your place overnight.

Put your plants back outside the next day but this time in an area of dappled sunlight. You know that romantic shade that has just enough sunlight to make your picnic partner look oh-so-appealing. Again, let them hang out all day and bring them back inside before sunset.

Day three is the same as day two, but if you can, put your plants in the full sun for a few hours and then back into that romantic dappled shade. Again, they all need to be back inside before the sun sets.

Keep repeating this pattern over the course of a week. Ideally, you will have a warm but overcast day to transplant your seedlings, but as you can expect, this does not happen very often, if at all.

So, Saturday has finally come around and you are finally ready to move all your plants into the garden. The first step is to prepare their future home. Remove any debris and other unwanted items from the garden bed and using a hand trowel or your fingers, make a hole in the soil a couple inches across and deep. You don't need to remove this soil, just push it to the side as it will be used to help bed the seedling. Once you have created the hole, sprinkle it with water. You want to make sure that the bottom of the hole is damp, but not soaked.

You can now focus on your seedling. Now, this does require care, so take your time until you get the hang of it. If you damage the roots of the seedlings, they may experience transplant shock, which can set them back a week or more. If the root damage is severe, your plants may die.

# Transplant Shock

The other term that we need to explain is "transplant shock." This is the adverse reaction that a plant can have either to changes in its environment, such as, increased temperature swings; physical damage such as having sections broken off; or even just being disturbed more than it is used to, such as, when the roots are disturbed during transplanting.

Given the need to move your plants outside, they will experience some level of transplant shock but there are some techniques to help reduce them.
Using your hand trowel, carefully cut the soil around the seedling and lift the soil from underneath the roots. Using your other hand to brace the small plant, lower the soil and its roots into the hole you just made in the garden. Doing your best to not touch or disturb the roots, place the seedling in its new home.

Using your hands, gently pack the soil that you pushed aside to fill the hole. This will put the soil around the stalk of the seedling. Again, being gentle, press the soil down. You are not aiming to flatten it all out, just to make sure that it is packed a little bit and is giving support to the lower section of the seedling stalk.

If you are putting more seedlings in this section of the garden, then simply repeat the process until you are finished. Once you have all the seedlings in their new home, sprinkle the soil again with water.

You have now done the most hazardous step. To give all your plants the best chance to survive, make sure the soil is kept moist until your plants are established.

But how can you tell when your plants are established? That is a good question, and this time it has a simple answer. Your plants will be standing tall, with no drooping stems or stalks and some new leaves appearing. When you see the first new set of leaves appear, you can pivot from a light sprinkling of the soil every day to the watering schedule best suited for your plants and your lifestyle.

I know that when you read through this section it may sound difficult and hard on the plants, but I am confident after you have gotten your first three or four plants in their new homes you will understand what you need to do. And when that flash of understanding shows up, and I know that it will. You've taken your first step on the road to becoming that wise gardener who effortlessly fills their entire pantry with food they've grown themselves.

# Chapter 15: Mulch

*"Do you see forest trees shatter into a zillion pieces and fall? No. They fall, then decompose, then spread."*
— Janet Macunovich

What is the deal with mulch? If you happen into a conversation with a gardener, there will be that momentary pause after you have discussed soil and composting, and you both take a sip of your drinks. You will look at each other, and then the question will pop out. So, what do you use to mulch your garden?

Before we dive into the specifics, we should talk about what it is.

An easy way to understand mulch is to think of it as a security blanket for your plants. Security blankets help create a higher level of confidence, give comfort and protection, as well as encouragement to grow and take on the challenges of life. So, when you add mulch to your garden, you are helping your plants get a leg up and start growing into their full potential.

Ok, enough artistic writing. Let me lay it out in simple terms, mulch performs several important jobs in your garden.

Firstly, it adds a layer of protection from weeds. Weeds can be started by seeds in the soil, coming from poorly rotted compost, or some other soil additives. When you cover your soil with mulch, you add more material for weed seedlings to grow up through to survive.

The other way that weeds can get established in your garden is from airborne seeds. These can be wind-blown such as dandelion fluff or dropped from the backend of a bird. Regardless of the source of the seeds, when they land on mulch and not soil, they do not find the triggers that start them germinating.

Secondly, when you add mulch to your garden you moderate the temperature of the soil and the roots living in that soil. Why does this matter? Like us, plants get uncomfortable when they get too hot. The transpiration of moisture through the leaves will help keep the portions of the plant above the soil cool and comfortable. But when the sun comes out on those great summer days, the soil heats up.

Much like moving under the shade of a sun tarp, the layer of mulch keeps the direct sun off the soil and the temperature down. The mulch also acts as a heat sink for the evening and overnight to help keep the soil temperature a bit warmer than it would be otherwise.

Finally, when you add a layer of mulch to your garden you help trap moisture in the soil. As we have already mentioned, most plants prefer to live in a consistently moist environment. They don't like to dry out and then be drowned every few days.

By mulching your garden, you keep the evaporation down to a minimum, so the moisture you so painstakingly add to your garden is available to your plant roots. Not only will this reduce the frequency of your watering, but mulch will also moderate the moisture levels and keep your plants much happier.

And as you know by now, when you can keep your plants happy, they will grow faster. To paraphrase a popular sentiment, "happy plant happy life."

## Types of Mulch

So, what can you use for mulch? Well pretty much anything you want, within reason of course.

Just like fertilizer, mulch is primarily divided into two major categories: organic and inorganic. I am sure some of you are thinking that really, there is no need to bother with the inorganic mulches. The organic ones will decompose over time and add even more nutrients to the soil, making them the obvious choice.

Given this, why would you even spend the time to learn about inorganic mulch? Bear with me as I go through them, and while you may decide to not use them, it can only help in your overall understanding of mulch.

### *Inorganic*

As you will have come to expect, an inorganic mulch does not contain anything organic.

### **Gravel and Stone**

These are natural, but not organic, products. I am pretty sure we have all seen the public parks and business frontages that are covered in a mix of rocks.

Using rocks as mulch is more suited for permanent landscaping and hardscaping than for a backyard garden. I am sure I do not need to go into the reasons why, but I am going to do just that, mostly because I can.

If you are planning to use gravel or stone for your mulch, be sure you will never need to adjust your soil, as trying to remove all the mulch is a lesson in aggravation. Just pause a moment to look at this picture: A hot sunny day in the middle of summer and your compost is ready to be spread in your garden for that midseason boost.

I know I would not want to spend the day collecting all the rocks or gravel just to put it all back once the compost is spread.

So, I'll say it again, gravel and rocks make ideal mulch if you are setting up a permanent landscaped area.

## Plastic Sheeting

There is no real way to claim that anything plastic is a natural product, so we are firmly into inorganic mulches. Plastic. There are many reasons not to use this in your garden, including the environmental impact, the pollution created when you pull it all out of your garden, and the fact the sun will destroy plastic sheeting in a year or less.

So, is there any reason to use plastic sheeting? Only one worth mentioning is weed control. Now I am not suggesting you put down plastic sheeting in your garden to kill the weeds. No. I am suggesting plastic sheeting can be used to kill a patch of lawn or weeded area you are planning to use as a garden.

When you spread out the plastic sheeting on the grass or weeds, it will trap the heat of the sun and raise the soil temperature high enough to kill pretty much any plant unlucky enough to be there. The plastic will also suffocate anything that has not been killed by the extreme heat and dehydrate the rest by blocking out all moisture.

## Rubber

Commonly found in parks and play areas, rubber mulch is typically made from recycled tires and other consumer rubber products. This material falls into the same category as gravel in that it is a great ground cover and a good weed barrier but is a pain to remove if you ever need to do anything with the underlying soil.

With that in mind, you might ask when would you use it and why have I included it? Rubber mulch is ideal around larger plants as it will reduce the impact of weeds and help keep the moisture in the soil.

Rubber mulch has the unique benefit of not being painful. When you layer it a couple of inches thick, it is soft to walk or work on. I am sure you can now see a few more applications for this material. What about as a covering for the ground around your raised-bed garden boxes? Or perhaps to cover the walkways around your in-ground garden so you have something soft to kneel on when you are weeding?

If you just look at the layout and arrangement of your garden area, I am confident you will find potential uses for this material. Typically, it can be a direct replacement for gravel without the bruises and discomfort that comes with gravel.

## Weed Barrier

This is the final selection in our survey of inorganic mulch materials. If you have been in a commercial garden supply store or nursery, there is a good chance you have been walking on a weed barrier of some sort.

Woven out of plastic, weed barrier or landscape fabric is the go-to choose for weed control for large areas. This fabric comes on rolls and in various thicknesses.

The benefits of using a weed barrier fabric lie not only in weed control, which this material is quite effective at, but also its secondary properties. Weed barrier fabric allows moisture to pass both ways, which will allow the soil underneath to maintain a correct moisture level.

Additionally, the open weave in the fabric does not interfere with air movement in and out of the soil.

By allowing both water and air to still interact with the soil, the weed barrier keeps the microorganisms living in the soil alive, while blocking out the weeds.

If you may someday have to return your garden to lawn, such as in a rental situation using a fabric-based weed barrier will make that transition as easy as possible. Simply pull up the fabric, rake the surface well, and scatter lawn seed and the grass will come back with little to no fuss.

As you imagine if you had used gravel, rock, or rubber mulch, you would be picking up the small pieces for some time before you could seed the lawn. It would be even worse if you had put down plastic sheeting. The plastic would have killed all the life in the soil that it covers. To bring the soil back to life enough to support a lawn and get your damage deposit back, you would need to replace the dirt with a decent topsoil before seeding your replacement lawn.

Now that we have covered the most common inorganic mulches, their uses, and drawbacks, we will turn our gaze to the world of organic mulches and join the rest of the gardeners in the never-ending debate and discussion as to which is the best.

## *Organic Mulch*

You know how this works by now. Organic mulches come from an organic source. These are typically renewable in some fashion, tend to be whatever is readily available locally, and will eventually decompose back into the soil as a form of compost.

So, what are we talking about here? The list of organic materials that can be used as mulch is limitless, provided it is not from allelopathic plants which contain chemicals that will kill most plants they encounter. Steer clear of any black walnut-based mulch. Additionally, do not grow a garden near any black walnut trees.

If you happen to be in a situation where you have access to evergreen tree material for mulch, you will need to think carefully before you apply it. As we have already mentioned, the plants in your garden have a pH range that they are the happiest in. For example, beets like to grow in a pH between 6.0 and 7.5, while tomatoes prefer between 5.5 and 7.5, and potatoes like between 4.5 and 6.0. Now, when you apply any type of organic mulch, it will affect the pH of the soil beneath it. I am singling out evergreen-based mulch because it will alter the soil pH to such a detrimental extent that your plants may be stunted or die. The pH of the soil under an evergreen-based mulch will eventually be reduced to between 4.5 and 5.0.

## Bark or Wood Chips

This can usually be found in bags or in a large pile at your local garden supply store. Another source for woodchip mulch is landscaping companies or tree surgeons. If you are not happy with the options available at your local nursery or garden supply store, spend a few minutes on the internet and find your local landscaping and tree removal companies. Some tree surgeons may let you have the mulch for free. They will have a good idea what type of trees the chips came from. Landscaping companies will also have either a supply of wood chip mulch or will be able to direct you to their preferred supplier.

Keeping in mind the significance of any evergreen tree material, ask to make sure you know what has been chipped to make the mulch. Most hardwood trees will decompose into a pH neutral material that is helpful for your garden. If your garden center does not know what is in the wood chip mulch, be reluctant to use it around your plants.

This material can still make great cover and keep the mud and weeds at bay there but might not be the ideal solution for your garden.

If you are going to use wood chip mulch for your garden, keep in mind that the chips will be almost as difficult to manage for soil modifications as if you had used gravel. However, you do not need to remove all the wood chips from the soil, as any that you miss will compost and become part of the nutrients for the plants.

## Straw Or Hay

This is the most desired mulch for the soil around your annuals. Not only will straw or hay keep errant weeds at bay, but it will also help retain moisture in the soil and help reduce pests. The details about how this works will be covered in the chapter on pests. Straw has the added benefit of having a benign effect on the soil when it composts.

The nature of straw means you can cover your garden soil with an inch or two of this type of mulch and leave it on the soil over the winter. It is simple to brush it aside when you need to remove a harvested plant or when you need to plant your spring seedlings.

Straw and hay will readily allow rain or other water to pass through into the soil but keep the now moist soil protected from heat during the day. The only drawback of using straw as a mulch is that it is lightweight. If you live in an area that gets gusty winds, it may tend to blow the straw around the garden. To resolve this messy problem, all you need is some chicken wire or other small, meshed fencing wire to lay on top of the straw. This mesh has the added benefit of keeping larger pests such as cats and racoons at bay, but we will get into more detail on this in the chapter on pests as well.

There are several sources of straw or hay, depending on how close you live to the country. If you are near a rural farming area, there will be ranching supply stores that will have bales of straw marketed as animal bedding. The other option is your local pet store.

## Fallen Leaves

Another common mulch is all those fallen leaves that accumulate in your yard. The primary problem with fallen leaves is that they only tend to fall after the harvest has been done and you are deep into the winter preparations.

So, what do you do if you want to use all those fallen leaves as a mulch? Simply collect as much as you want in the fall and compost it until you are ready to use it during the summer growing season. If you have the space to pile all the leaves in your yard somewhere, they will be ready to use when you need then.

I know that if someone came to my place and wanted to collect and take away all my fallen leaves, I would even offer to rake them all into a pile for them. The upside of asking your neighbors for their leaves is that not only will you get to meet everyone on your block, you will find out how many of them are also gardeners.

With all your leaves in a pile and they have started to compost over the winter, they are ready for use. Once you have all your seedlings in the soil, spread out the partially composted leaves about an inch or two deep and you will have all the mulch you will need for the season.

## Grass Clippings

If you are paying attention, and I am sure you are, then you will be wondering about lawn clippings. Not only are these available throughout the summer, but a hassle also to dispose of, and you get more every week when you mow your lawn, you might wonder if you can use all that as mulch.

Well, that depends. I know that is a bit of a cop-out but let me explain. When you use grass clippings as mulch, you must realize it is very high in water. This extra moisture will result in a wet, slimy surface on the clippings. Not only this not very nice to look at, but it will also generate some unpleasant odors.

When the grass starts to compost it tends to form a solid mat that prevents water from penetrating, and eventually harms the soil until the grass clippings are fully composted.

Ideally, you would add all your grass clippings and those of your neighbors if you are short of clippings, into your compost. This will add plenty of nutrients and minerals to the compost that will be ready for the following summer.

## Newspaper

If you live in an area that still has printed newspapers, you can use them as mulch.

The simplest approach is to lay out the pages on your soil while making sure that you do not cover any plants. This can be easier if you shred the newsprint first, but you will need to cover this shredded material with something to keep the wind from blowing it around, if you live in a windy area.

Ideally, you would layer an inch or two of paper, and this should last the growing season, but it is also perfectly fine to add more during the summer as needed.

Once you have harvested your garden in the fall, you can cover the newsprint and it will tend to compost over the winter and become part of the soil for the next season The one drawback to newsprint, besides the availability, is that it makes an almost perfect environment for airborne or dropped seeds to germinate. An inch of newsprint will stop all soil-based seeds from germinating but do not be surprised to find weeds starting on top after a few weeks.

.

# Cardboard

As a close relative to newsprint, many people use cardboard as mulch. This works very well if you are looking to kill off a section of lawn and turn it into a garden plot. In fact, using cardboard can be as effective as plastic sheeting for killing part of your lawn.

It has the bonus of not needing to be removed when you want to start your garden. Simply pile your soil on top and get gardening. The cardboard will compost in a year or two and add what little minerals and nutrients it has to your soil.

You can use cardboard as a soil mulch if you are willing to spend the time to make sure it fits around your plants. If you do this, be aware that the cardboard will absorb a great deal of water and you will need to make sure that enough is getting past to keep your plants properly moist.

We have looked at a large variety of materials that can and have been used for mulch and discussed the benefits and drawbacks of each of them. Hopefully, this has given you an idea of what a good mulch is intended to do, how to pick a material that will work for you.

Take your time to assess any material that you are debating to use as a mulch. Will it harm your plants? What about the soil underneath? How will it affect the water? If you conclude it will work for you, then use it. This is all part of your journey to becoming a gardener.

# Chapter 16: Companion Gardening

*"My garden is my most beautiful masterpiece."*
-Claude Monet

We have already looked at what are the most common plants to grow in your garden. We have not looked at is which plants grow well together, which ones will get in each other's way, and which ones just don't care who they live beside.

The topic of which plants play well with each other is known as companion planting. You are looking for plants that will help each other grow and can coexist in the same space. You can look at this from several different viewpoints. You may want all the plants in a garden bed to look pleasing together. Maybe you have a specific soil pH profile you want to use and need plants that like the same pH. Perhaps you want a vertical garden, so you need to know which plants can grow in the shade of others, or you want to manage pests and attract pollinators. You may simply want to get the most harvest possible from your garden.

As you can see, there are many reasons why you would need to know how plants interact. These combinations can be divided into short-and long-term effects.

Let's take basil as an example of a short-term beneficial companion plant. It will attract most of the aphids that happen across your garden. Yes, the idea is to plant basil to let them get infested. As your basil plants succumb to the aphids, they will be sacrificed to save the rest of your garden.

Companion planting tends to be the most effective with a longer-term view of your garden. While there may not be as many benefits in the first year or two, if you continue to garden with companion planting, you will soon start to see an increase not only in your harvest yields but a reduction of the common garden pests.

## Friends Help Friends Grow

Now we all have a circle of friends. I am sure some of your friends will not get along with others in your circle, yet they all get along with, and are important to you. The same idea can be applied to plants.

There are plants that are like the extrovert friend. Somehow, they are good in groups. Other friends interact best one-on-one.

When we look at a vibrant, healthy garden what we see is an expression of the relationships between the plants and the person looking after them. Not only do the plants in your garden need the correct water, soil, and light, they can become more than the sum of their parts if they are partnered with the correct plants.

On one hand this makes sense as we know that we are affected by who we surround ourselves with. But to realize that your plants can likewise also be affected is to begin to understand your plants better and better.

So, how do beneficial plants help each other?

### *Protection*

This is purely a physical benefit. If you plant your basil seedlings under the canopy of your tomato plants, the tomato plants can have all the bright sunshine they love while filtering out the harsh light for the more delicate basil that would suffer in the bright light.

There will be the added protection for the basil against any inclement weather. As your tomato plants are hardier than basil, they can take the abuse from that heavy summer rain or hail. Most of the tomato plant is not meant to be harvested, so the leaves and stalks can take some damage without affecting your harvest.

Let's go a little more complex. The growing of beans, corn, and squash does provide for a very balanced diet, with carbohydrates from the corn, protein from the beans, and additional minerals and vitamins in the squash. The difficulty in growing these three on their own is that the corn will tend to be knocked over in heavy winds, the beans need something to climb, and the squash will grow better if the soil is kept moist.

The understanding of the needs of these individual plants led to the innovation of the three sisters planting. All three of these plants are grown in the same garden patch. The corn grows quickly and provides a climbing surface for the slightly slower growing beans. In turn the beans intertwine between the corn stalks and provide additional stability to the corn in the event of bad weather.

Both corn and beans tend to have narrower leaves. This allows a great deal of the sunlight to reach down to the squash plants. Squash will grow into whatever space they have available, and beyond if they can. While they can climb, they are far better suited as ground cover as they will grow more, and larger leaves, as they are exposed to more sunlight.

So, you can see that if the beans were left as ground cover, then they would be overwhelmed by the far more vigorous squash, but the corn stalks have given them an escape path.

The massive squash leaves not only help the squash grow better, but they also act as a natural form of mulch. The layering of these leaves will help keep as much moisture as possible in the soil, as well as keep down weeds that might try to compete with the three sisters.

But what about the beans? As they grow, the rhizomes in their roots pull nitrogen from the air and convert it into a form that the roots of the other plants can use. In effect, the beans are adding fertilizer to the soil as they grow.

Not everyone is willing to or has the space to grow the three sisters in their garden, but it provides a great example of the benefits of companion planting.

### *Pests*

Bullies will tend to identify and pick on the weakest member of a group if they can. There will be less resistance. The same can be said of pests that are attracted to your garden plants. They will go after most any plant they can find, but they will always prefer certain plants over others.

When you use companion planting as part of your pest control strategy, you are letting the natural features of your plants do most of the heavy lifting.

As we mentioned earlier, basil is commonly used as a sacrificial plant to attract the aphids and spider mites away from other plants you want to grow. Well, that is great, unless you happen to want to grow your basil plants for you, and not just to feed the aphids. In this case, you could surround your patch of basil with marigolds that not only look good but are effective at repelling aphids.

Now, there are about as many pests as there are plants that you might want to grow, possibly even more. So how can companion planting help? There are a couple broad categories to look at here:

### Attracting other pests

If you know there are pests in your garden, or you want to try and keep them away, perhaps you can attract some other insect or creature that will help to deal with these pests and not harm your plants.

The most common way to do this is to bring in ladybugs. Did you know they can be ordered either from your local garden supply house or online? They will ignore your plants as they hunt aphids.

There are types of wasps and bees that can help with pest control, as well as with pollinating your plants. There are birds that will come and eat the insects in your garden, moths and butterflies that see your plants as a free buffet, and burrowing creatures that will increase the quality of your soil while they devour problem creatures like hookworms and slugs.

We will cover the details of all these beneficial insects, and how to attract them when we get to pest control in the next chapter, but for now you need to know that with some pre-planning you can use your plants to not only create your food and a beautiful garden space, but also keep pests away.

### Deterring

In addition to attracting other creatures to feed on your pests, you can plant specific plants that will repel them from even setting up home in the first place.

Conveniently, there are many herbs that most people like to eat that will also act as pest deterrents. The most common of these are mint, tansy, dill, parsley, fennel, thyme, and cilantro.

I know that cilantro will divide people, but if you are among those who do not like it, the fact it will help keep away pests might swing it a bit into your good books.

You can also plant a border of flowers around your garden if you have the space. Not only will this add a nice aesthetic, but it can also help keep pests at bay. The most common flowers used for this are nasturtiums, chrysanthemums, petunias, and marigolds. So perhaps this is just the excuse you needed to add some pretty flowers to your vegetable garden?

## Enemies

Now that we have looked at how plants can be beneficial for each other, we need to look at how and when plants try to kill each other in your garden, or at a minimum, make life difficult for each other.

## Common Attractants

When plants share common pests, they should not be planted together. For example, corn and tomatoes are both susceptible to similar worms and fungus blights. If you plant both in the same garden patch and one of them happens to attract a worm or a fungus, there is a good chance it will spread to all the plants just because they are so close together.

Keeping this in mind when you design your garden will help eliminate these potential problems, as you now know to plant your corn and tomatoes at different ends of the garden.

## Inhibitors

If you are going to plant deterrent plants, such as garlic and fennel, you would be best served to have them either in their own beds, or even better, in containers that can be moved around if you have a pest infestation that has somehow managed to get past all your defenses.

## Nutrient Theft

Neither potato nor zucchini have a problem with each other, so you would think that they could be planted in the same garden bed. After all, the potatoes are tubers and their above ground plant does not take up much space, while zucchini are all above ground, have huge leaves, and spread as far as you let them.

Now, this sounds like a perfect way to double up on the productivity of your garden, but it would be a mistake. The problem comes with their appetites. While zucchinis are content to take only what they need from the soil, potatoes are the buffet hog that you don't want in front of you.

If you happen to try and grow these two in the same plot, the potatoes will likely do well at the expense of the zucchini that will have been starved for minerals and nutrients.

## What Is That?

One of the more peculiar reasons to be careful which plants that you grow in the same beds is the chance of cross-pollination. The most common mistake people make is to plant both pumpkins and squash in the same bed.

At first glance this is a perfectly reasonable thing. They have very similar soil, water, and light requirements. They are both ground-based vines with heavy fruit, they can cover areas that might otherwise be of no value as a garden.

There are two problems with this, however. They both can grow enormous leaves, they will compete for sunlight, but this can be resolved by pruning any leaves that get carried away.

The other problem cannot be fixed. When it comes to pollinating, pumpkins and squash are similar enough they pollinate each other's flowers. Unless you are hand pollinating each flower, you have no control over where the pollen comes from. While this is not the end of the world, it can end up with you growing a very peculiar hybrid pumpkin/squash gourds that might make you wonder just what on earth happened last summer.

Typically, these hybrid gourds will be edible, but you can never know what they will look and taste like. Unless you are interested in plant husbandry, I suggest you plant your pumpkins and squash as far apart as you can.

## Everyone Into the Pool

If you are worried about all these details and possible interactions, please be reassured that most plants are self-centered enough to not care what grows around them. As you would expect.

So, why bother with all the discussion about companion planting if you can simply put whatever plants, you want together in the same garden plot or container? Primarily, it is to explain why some plants will grow better or worse in different locations.

It is perfectly feasible to put the plants you want to grow where you want them to grow and then look after them. Most of the time everything will work out quite well. When you look through the growing guides, you will find a section on companion planting. If you do not see the plant combination you are interested in, it can be safe to assume there are no commonly known problems with planting them together.

This should take some of the pressure off as you make all the pieces of the plant jigsaws fit together. As you have seen, there are an almost endless number of factors that can be considered when you plant your plants, but often, everything will grow even if you ignore everything we have discussed so far.

Before you go freeform in your garden, keep in mind you are growing a garden to produce food to eat. By following the suggestions regarding companion planting, you can both reduce the amount of work you have to do, which is a good thing in my view, as well as increase the yield from your plants.

# Pollinators

What do birds, butterflies, beetles, and bees have in common besides a love of the letter "b?"

They are all pollinators. Now, I am sure there are some of you who know of other fascinating commonalities, but for now, we will limit our conversation to pollination.

As there is never a stupid question, I am going to give a brief overview of pollination. If you already know this, then humor me for a moment. If you are not sure what we are talking about, or just need some reassurance that what you think you know is correct, the next couple paragraphs are for you.

Pollination is basically sex for plants. I am going to assume that we all know how sex works. Good.

When it comes to plants and sex, they are unable to make those smooth comments, accidentally touch each other, or bring out the wine and spin up the smooth jazz. Instead, they must rely on the birds, butterflies, beetles, and bees to get the business done for them.

To entice these enablers, plants have fancy looking flowers to appeal to their aesthetics, sweet nectar on tap for those with a sweet tooth, and resting places for those that have exhausted themselves in the execution of their duties. The list of pollinators is just a starting point. as there may be many other types of creatures attracted to the nectar or wide leaf resting places.

So, how does the sex life of your plants affect you? Well, this is the primary method that your plants use to produce your harvest, unless you are just growing leafy greens. The pollination of your plants is also required if you are planning to harvest some seeds for next year.

When you are staring at that huge display of seeds at your local nursery or garden supply store, you will see labels on the packages proclaiming the seeds to be F1, or heirloom, or more commonly, there is nothing beyond the plant name.

The F1 Hybrids are produced by the cross-pollination of two plants. And before you ask, what this means is the F1 Hybrid seeds have been designed over years of plant selection and pollination to produce a plant with specific properties.

These may be a tomato that is as large as a melon, or cherry tomatoes that look like a bunch of grapes, or carrots that are the proper carrot shape. Whatever the property the horticulturist wanted to create will be in the F1 Hybrid seeds. Keep in mind that this is not a

genetically modified seed. The properties are expressed in the plant they grow have been selected by careful pollination and not gene-splicing.

The advantage of F1 Hybrid seeds is they typically produce a self-pollinating plant that often will be a high producer. Sounds great, doesn't it? But as with everything in life there is a downside. If you grow F1 based plants through to seed production, there is no guarantee, or even expectation that those seeds will grow into the same plant they came from. F1 hybrids are intended to be grown from new store-bought seeds each year.

That brings us to the last variety of seeds, heirloom.

Heirloom seeds will grow into plants that will produce seeds that will again grow into the same plant, again and again and again. It is these heirloom plants that have formed the basis of human agriculture since we first learned to farm.

Heirloom plants are what we think of when we grow our plants. I mean who really wants to be beholden to a seed company to provide you with seeds every year when you are growing plants that make their own seeds?

But, of course, there are drawbacks to growing heirloom seeds. The produce they grow will on average be smaller and fewer than that produced by an F1 hybrid. You may need to grow an extra plant or two to make up the harvest difference, and if you have the space, this is a simple solution. For those of you with more limited growing space, the benefits of an F1 hybrid might outweigh the drawbacks.

Now we can get to pollinator attracting plants. If you are growing heirloom seeds, you will need pollinators to fertilize the flowers and get the plant to produce the fruit you are looking to harvest. If the plant is not pollinated, it will not produce viable seeds to use next year either.

There are several methods to bring enough pollinators into your garden to make sure all your plants are happy and ready to go: You could become a beekeeper and have your own backyard hives. You could create a perfect replica of a local field or forest

102

and let the pollinators take over, but this might take a decade or two. More practically, you can grow certain plants and design your garden area to make it attractive to pollinators.

To me the last option sounds the most feasible. But what does that really mean? Well, if you let the area around your garden accumulate some leaf litter and other natural debris, you are giving the pollinator somewhere safe to land and rest. Combining this with plants like borage that is almost irresistible to bees, and some bird baths kept filled with water, your garden will become the hot hangout in the neighborhood.

And trust me, these are the characters you want hanging around your yard. To attract as many pollinators as you can, consider planting any or all the following plants:

- Herbs
    - Basil, Dill, Parsley, Thyme, Sage.
    - Attracts Butterflies, Bees, Hummingbirds
- Lantana
    - Attracts Butterflies
- Fuchsia
    - Attracts Hummingbirds
- Sweet Alyssum
    - Attracts Butterflies, Bees
- Sunflowers
    - Attracts Butterflies
- Calendula
    - Attracts Bees
- Catmint
    - Attracts Butterflies, Hummingbirds, Bees
- Dahlia
    - Attracts Butterflies, Bees
- Borage
    - Attracts Bees
- Daisy
    - Attracts Butterflies, Bees
- Lavender
    - Attracts Bees
- Marigold
    - Attracts Bees

This is by no means an exhaustive list of plants that will attract pollinators, but it is a good starting point. If by chance you do not find any plants on that list that are appealing, ask the staff at your local garden supply store or plant nursery next time you are there. They will have a good idea as to what most people are growing and perhaps there will be a plant or two of interest for you.

One final note on planting pollinator attracting plants: It is worth the effort and time. There are not many things worse than spending the summer tending and caring for your plants only to find that they produce almost nothing come harvest time.

Pollinators equal produce.

# Chapter 17: Care

*"The glory of gardening: hands in the dirt, head in the sun, heart with nature. To nurture a garden is to feed not just the body, but the soul."*

– Alfred Austin

Well, it has been a few words and a few chapters, but we have finally gotten to the meat of the book: Growing your own food. We have looked at what plants to grow, how to layout your garden or raised beds or containers and how to germinate seeds. We then took some time to discuss how to make your soil perfect for your plants, when and how to water them, what compost and fertilizer means and how to use them, and then we looked at which plants to put together and why that makes a difference.

Now, here we are. You have all your seeds or seedlings in their summer homes and now you need to get them through the summer and all the way to harvest.

There are some people who will skip this chapter and get onto pest control and dealing with weeds, thinking that caring for plants involves nothing more than watering them when they are dry. This is partially correct, as all plants do need water to keep them alive. But saying that caring for your plants only means watering when needed is like saying that all you need to worry about as an adult is having something to drink, and we all know that life is far more complicated than that.

Given that we are growing the garden to supply you with food during the summer and ideally over the winter as well, there are some things that are worth considering as the growing season gets going.

The first is yield. By this I do not mean the total harvest yield, though that will be a strong consideration when we look at how to store your harvest over the winter. What I am referring to is the weekly yield you can expect during the growing season.

Let's compare bell peppers and lettuce. Both plants will have been transplanted into your garden about the same time. Now, on average bell peppers will take between 60 and 90 days to grow from seed to a harvest-ready pepper. Lettuce on the other hand will take between 30 and 70 days.

That means it is possible to have a lettuce harvest every six weeks, while you can only expect a pepper harvest every two-and-a-half to three months. But I am sure that you would like to enjoy a fresh salad more than once during the summer.

The solution to this dilemma is a concept called "staggered planting." This is where purchasing and transplanting some seedlings from your local nursery can be very helpful. Seeing as these seedlings already have several weeks head start over your germinated seeds; they will be ready for harvest much sooner.

# Planting

When it comes to planting seeds and seedlings in the spring, most new gardeners fall into the same trap, and I know from experience just how easily that happens. In the excitement of your first spring as a gardener, you put all your plants in the garden and start looking after them.

What happens is in a month or two your lettuce plants are ready to be harvested. You suddenly find yourself with ten or more full heads of lettuce in your fridge. Well, it is salads every meal for the next week, and by the time you have eaten or given away the last head, you never want to see another lettuce plant again.

The same will happen when your green onions are ready, your bell peppers, and your cucumbers. Wouldn't it be far more satisfying to have all these available for your Sunday meal? It is possible, and it only requires some patience.

Trust me when I say this is an exercise that will cause you some stress initially but is most definitely worth it when you are able to fill your plate with a fresh salad every week.

So, what is the trick? Stagger your planting. I'll use lettuce as an example, but the same methodology applies to peppers, carrots, cucumbers, and pretty much everything else you might grow except indeterminate tomatoes.

## *Serial*

Ensuring you have a head of lettuce ready for harvest each week is as simple as planting a new lettuce seedling or two every week. In the first weeks of the season, you can plant some lettuce seedlings from the nursery to give your seeds time to germinate and produce their true leaves.

The trick to effective staggered planting is to only plant enough new seedlings each week to meet the demand you have when they are ready for harvest. It is a good idea to plant a couple of extra seedlings in case there are pests or growth issues, but don't overdo it.

Try and get into the habit of taking time the same day each week to transplant a new seedling or two in your garden. After this, start a few more seeds germinating. This will ensure a continual supply of harvest-ready lettuce.

An often-overlooked advantage of serial planting is that you can reduce the overall space allocated to plants. You will be continually harvesting and replanting in the same soil throughout the season, effectively more than quadrupling your yield from that patch of soil.

The other approach to consider is a partial harvest. Lettuce, for example, a handful of leaves taken from each plant creates a salad, instead of harvesting an entire head. This will let the lettuce plants continue to grow, producing more leaves. You will need to watch for your lettuce plant trying to bolt, however. This is when the plant starts to produce a long, thin central stem which is the first step to producing seeds. At this point, you will need to harvest the entire head or let it go to seed, as the lettuce leaves will start to become more and more bitter with each passing day.

When it comes to peppers, it is easier to simply harvest the large ripe ones each week and let the rest continue to grow.

Look at the harvest times for each of the plants you want to grow and compare that to your expectations of what you want to have fresh over the summer. This will give you a good idea of the planting intervals you should aim for. With some careful planning, you can easily have a garden-fresh salad every week from plants you have grown yourself.

## *All At Once*

The other approach to planting is to have all the produce ripen at the same time. But why would you want to do this if you are spending the time to figure out serial planting for your summer salads?

To adequately explain the need for the two different harvest techniques, you need to understand that your garden can fulfill two very different needs at the same time.

The difference between serial planting and all-at-once planting is, as you would guess, in the names. You are either harvesting as you need throughout the season, or you are waiting until the end of the season at which time you will harvest everything, all at once.

When you are planning your garden for a large fall harvest, you will need some idea of how you plan to preserve your bounty. This may affect when the ideal harvest time is, which will cascade back to a specific start and transplanting time to make sure everything is ready when you want.

Can I give some examples? What says summer more than fresh tomatoes? Now, if you want to capture those glorious warm days to heat you in the depth of winter, there are a couple ways to preserve your harvest.

The first thing that comes to mind for most people will be to make some type of tomato sauce or paste. Now, don't get me wrong, these are both very good, but there is a better way.

If you have never tried a sun-dried tomato, I suggest you splurge on a jar and find a recipe that you like. Those of us that know the wonder that you are about to experience will wait for you to return before we continue this discussion.

Welcome back. So? Kinda blew your mind, I am thinking. All the heat and experience of that last summer packed into a simple bite on your fork. Now, the primary problem I have found with sun-dried tomatoes is the price. But here is where the timing on your garden comes into play.

If you live somewhere warm, you can very easily make your own sun-dried tomatoes. But obviously, to do this you need hot sunny days that are typical of late summer. So, it makes sense to look at the harvest time of your selected tomatoes and make sure you have started them with a week or two to spare.

I think that you are beginning to understand the idea here. Now, if in addition to the sun-dried tomatoes, you want to make some tomato sauce, paste, or simple canned tomatoes, it makes the most sense to have all the fruit come ripe all at the same time so you can do all the processing and work over a weekend instead of having to process a jar or two every few days.

Not only will this make the processing much simpler and faster, as you can bribe your friends to help you and make the work into an event, you will have a more consistently ripe product to preserve, which will make the final product tastier.

Take a moment and give some thought as to how you imagine the fall harvest and how much food you would ideally be storing, as this will influence how you manage your garden during the summer.

The same planting and harvesting approach will work for herbs and most other plants that you grow.

# Pruning

Pruning your plants can serve several purposes from aesthetics, disease, and pest control, to increasing the harvest yield. So why are so many people against pruning if it can be so helpful?

The most common answer is that they do not know what they are doing and are scared to do it wrong and either kill the plants or do something that will affect the harvest.

This is a good answer. If you go crazy and cut off most of the branches from your tomato plants then yes, you will not have a very happy plant, or a bountiful harvest. However, if you are growing an indeterminate variety of tomato and prune it correctly, you will not only increase the quality of the fruit, but you will also increase your harvest yields.

Sounds too good to be true. And that is what I believed, until I tried it. Now yes, I did make some mistakes and grew a few incredibly green and lush plants that didn't produce a single tomato. I aim to help you learn from my mistakes so you can have a garden that not only looks great, but also is productive.

If you are only concerned about plant growth, there is no need to prune anything, and you can just let the plants go crazy. They will likely produce something for you to harvest, and may end up looking a bit messy, but not everyone has the time nor inclination to prune and manicure garden plants.

Another reason to prune your garden plants is aesthetics. I had the pleasure of working with a Japanese gardener for a few years. When he pruned his plants, he not only made sure to manage the plants for maximum productivity, but he also sculpted them into works of art. There is a fine line between pruning your plants and damaging them. The best method to learn the science, and art, of pruning is to talk to your local horticulturalist. Most garden supply stores will be able to direct you to the local authority. Social media is flooded with people claiming to know how to prune all types of plants but until you have a sufficient understanding of the process, it is best to get your advice from an expert, in person.

Once you understand the rationale behind pruning you will quickly realize there is no separation between functional pruning for increasing harvest yields, and aesthetic pruning. If you are inclined, you can sculpt and shape your plants to please your style and eye without decreasing the harvest yield. In fact, if you apply the right pruning techniques to your sculpting, along with creating something beautiful to look at, you can reduce diseases, pests, and increase your harvest. And before you know it, you will have become addicted to your garden.

## Support

We all have that friend that says they'll support us in whatever we do. Now, unless you are still a child at heart, which would be fantastic, it is unlikely that you will take them up on their words and have them carry you about.

As we grow up, we come to understand that they mean they can provide emotional, technical, or financial support rather than true physical support. But here is the important bit, your plants need that physical support. Well, not all of them to be true, but it sounded better.

The vast majority of plants you are likely to grow will be able to support themselves as they get started. Of course, there are vine type plants such as cucumbers that need support to grow properly.

Over the last centuries, we have also been selecting the varieties of the plants we grow based on productivity, and not structural integrity.

What this means is all the care and attention you have given your plants by making sure they have enough light, the correct soil, and even the right amount of water will get them producing fruit.

Now, the correct support will differ for each plant. Some, such as vine-based cucumbers or indeterminate tomatoes, will need a sturdy structure they can climb on and grow over. Other plants, such as your bell peppers, might just need a stick that the stalk can lean against.

As your plants grow, you will see where and what type of support they need. But before you head off to your local DIY store, remember you cannot use anything that has been pressure-treated or galvanized. The chemicals in the pressure treating and the zinc in the galvanizing will slowly poison your plants every time you water them, or they get rain.

Plants supports are another area where your personal style and aesthetic can shine. The only thing that the support needs to do is to help hold up your plants, and not poison them in the process, so your support can be as crazy and wild as you like, or as simple as a single piece of wooden dowelling. Personalize your garden. It is your space, and being in that space should make you happy. If that means families of faeries and garden gnomes, fountains and pathways paved with broken ceramic mosaics, or pared down modern minimalism, then so be it. It is totally and utterly up to you.

## Pollinating

We touched on the importance of attracting pollinators when we discussed companion planting, so I am confident you realize that even if you are not a great fan of all those creatures and insects in your garden, we do need them around.

Saying that, it is possible for you to assist or replace pollinators with a bit of work and a Q-tip. I strongly recommend you take the time to attract as many pollinators as you can with your plants and companion planting as this will, in the long run, reduce the amount of work that you need to do, and who doesn't like the sound of that?

Once you have all your plants growing, flowers will start appearing, and unless you are growing herbs, this is a good sign that your garden is progressing well.

Before I forget, if you are growing herbs and see flowers starting to form, you need to pinch or cut them off, unless you are growing that plant for seeds. In the case of herbs, the presence of the flowers changes the taste of the leaves, and usually not for the better. You can keep removing the flowers from your herbs until the frost kills the plant.

Right, back to the flowers. Once the flowers open, they will start to attract the pollinators. Once they have done their thing, the flowers will drop their petals and you will start to see the fruit develop. If you see that the flower petals have dropped and nothing starts to develop, odds are good that the flower was not pollinated.

There is nothing that can be done for the current flower, but as the new ones open, this is your opportunity to step up. With your Q-tip or similar device in hand, investigate the flower. We are going to get a bit technical here, to make sure you understand what you are looking at.

To pollinate the flower you will need to collect some of the pollen and rub it onto the top of the stigma. Once you have spread out the pollen, you can head to the next flower and repeat. This needs to be done to every flower on the plant, and ideally, every day until the petals drop. Make sure that you change the Q-tip to a new one when you switch to a different plant. You can see how tedious this would be to do to all your plants, thus the importance of attracting as many pollinators as possible.

## Weeding

Regardless of how you see weeding, you know in your heart that it is not fun. And no, I am not talking about hiring a gardener to do it for you.

We have already covered the importance of mulch. So, that was the first tip. For effective weed control, make sure you have a good layer, between one and three inches of mulch on your soil. This will create a significant barrier to weeds.

The next tip is to not leave any soil uncovered. If you have a section of the garden that is not in use this year, cover the soil with mulch or compost, something that will deter unwanted weeds.

And the last tip? Well, I almost hate to say it, but learn to like weeding.

Understanding that weeds are simply plants growing where you do not want them will open your eyes to the possibility that any plant can be a weed. Having watched your seedlings germinate, grow the cotyledon leaves, and then their true leaves, you know that the leaves you find as weeds emerge likely bear no resemblance to the final true leaf form, and as such, cannot be used for weed identification.

So how do you know what is a weed and what is not? Well, this is where all your planning comes to the rescue. You know that you planted your tomato seedlings in a row in that bed, that your carrots are in a row near the front, and that your potato plants are in a grid starting at the far corner of their plot.

In these instances, it pays to mark the row with a piece of string on a stick at each end. This way you can readily identify plants that are not in the carrot row. At this point, you will see a row of like-shaped leaves. Any plant that has a different-shaped leaf is a weed.

This all sounds good on the page, but I am sure some of you will be concerned you might pull out one of your plants thinking it is a weed. And you will. But this is known as thinning. When you seed carrots, for example, you will usually add several seeds at each location to make sure that at least one germinates. If you accidentally weed the first one, well, you should still have one or two more coming along to replace it.

If it turns out that you accidentally pulled them all up, then simply replant and start again. Chalk it up to learning. I am pretty sure that you will not do it a second time.

What else can I say about weeding? Keep your eyes open. Make sure to pull the weeds.

# Chapter 18: Pest Control

*"Only bugs can truly appreciate the beauty of flowers."*

- Dov Davidoff

The good, the bad, and the ugly: There is an almost endless stream of pests that will try to attack your garden during the summer. So hard is the fight that it can be overwhelming. Don't let this deter you, however, as there are some techniques you can use to have your garden do most of the heavy lifting for you.

As we have mentioned, you can use companion planting intentional buffets for the pests and once they have all fallen for the bait, you can dispose of the plants and all their visitors. The correct choice of plants can also create a deterrent to keep most pests from ever showing up in the first place.

Now, I know there is a certain appeal to having a garden that is insect free. What could be better than a warm afternoon or evening in your garden where you are not bothered by mosquitos, where your plants are not being snacked on by legions of aphids, and your potatoes are blight free?

If you are looking for such a pristine growing environment, you might be better suited to the precise world of indoor hydroponics. But before you head down to your local grow-op supplier, you should know that growing your food with hydroponics is technical and demanding. Which has more appeal to you? An afternoon spent in your garden with a drink, wandering about and enjoying the sights, sounds, and smells of summer or putting on a lab coat and spending your afternoon surrounded by computers, bright lights, and the endless hum of fans and air filtration systems as you monitor the instrument readings?

Now that we have established your preference, and it is not hard to guess which one you chose. So, we need to accept that insects, birds, and other creatures are a required part of gardening. I am not asking you to suddenly become an entomologist and fill your home with exotic spiders. I simply want you to learn to let your garden function as it needs, even if some of the participants might give you nightmares and shivers. Unless you are willing to step up and do their work, it is easiest to let them play their part while you sip your drink and soak up the ambience.

# Good Bugs

I know this might seem impossible to believe, but there are good insects out there in the big world. The goal when it comes to insect management is to have as many beneficial ones as possible in your garden, while excluding the problematic ones. Kind of like your circle of friends. We like to surround ourselves with those who support us and help us grow as people, but there always seems to be a problematic friend or two who somehow manages to stick around. You know the one. Who else would suggest all those wild and crazy adventures? Now a couple friends like that are part of how we learn and decide the type of life we want to live, but too many, and well, you might not like where you end up.

Managing the pests in your garden is a similar undertaking. You want only a few bad eggs so that all the beneficial insects will continue to hang around and help. Too much control and you will find yourself alone, fighting off the bad influences.

Instead of a full scale strategy to attract all the good insects, I am going to touch on the most common beneficial insects you want to have in your garden, and plants that attract them. While there are millions of different insects in the world, there are only a handful that might cause you problems, and thankfully, many more that will help your garden if you can simply point them in the right direction.

### *Soldier Beetle*
A dark-shelled beetle with orange stripes on the belly, the soldier beetle is attracted to goldenrod, marigolds, and zinnias. As it wanders around your garden, not only will it help pollinate your flowers, but it will also do its best to eat every aphid and caterpillar that crosses its path.

### *Hoverfly*
Also known as Syrid Flies, these small flies can easily be spotted as they hover near their favorite plants. These small but hard-working helpers are attracted to bergamot, cosmos, dill, mint, parsley, and zinnias. They will consume all the aphids, caterpillars, mealybugs, and thrips that they can find.

### *Lady Bug*
That friendly childhood bug is in fact very helpful to have in your garden. They are attracted to the same plants as the hoverflies and the same food sources but have a distinct appetite

for aphids. The more ladybugs that you can get to stay in your garden, the better off you will be.

## *Stink Bug*

Ya, these guys got the short end of the stick when names were being chosen, but regardless, they are good to have around. They have a particular fondness for fruit trees but will typically come check out the offerings in your garden all the way from your neighbors' apple tree. They do love a good meal of aphids or caterpillars, so encourage them to come visit, just do your best not to squish them.

## *Lacewing*

Small, almost ephemeral flying green insects, lacewings are attracted to coriander, dill, fennel, and sunflowers. Once they have shown up, they will come out at night to hunt for aphids, mealy bugs, mites, and thrips.

## *Dragonflies and Damselflies*

Acrobatic masters of flight, these winged insects love a pond or a bird bath. In return, they will eat as many flies and mosquitoes as they can find. A mosquito-free backyard is a good deal in return for water.

## *Bees*

We've all seen the news articles about the decline in the bee population. This is not good news as they pollinate a huge portion of the plants that we consume. Their loss will have a significant impact on us, so we need to do our part to make sure they have a food supply, even in the urban centers where people now live.

To bring these hardworking pollinators to your garden, plant basil, cucumbers, dill, mint, oregano, peas, rosemary, or borage. Any or all these not only add to the possibilities in your kitchen, but they also bring in bees that are in the neighborhood.

## *The Rest*

I am not going to bore you with page after page of bugs and how they are helpful, beyond the common ones I have already mentioned. There are so many, I would never finish listing them here. Instead, I am going to leave the discussion around good bugs with this thought.

If your plants are happy and healthy looking, and you're not finding many of the problematic bugs that I will cover next, let all the insects and other creatures that you find just get on with their lives. They might be doing your garden some good, or they might simply be passing through. Either way, they are not doing any harm. Learn to enjoy the diversity of creatures that come to check out your garden.

# Bad Bugs

While there are millions of insects that might cause problems for you, there are only a handful of insects commonly known as "bad ones." They will eat the leaves, suck out the juices, and cut the roots of the plants you are working so hard to nurture.

## *Aphid*

Top of the list of most common, and most annoying pests are aphids. These little creatures, smaller than a grain of rice, can be green, brown, black, and possibly many other colors depending on where you live. They typically cluster on the underside of leaves. Aphids suck the sap from your plants, literally sucking out their lifeblood every moment of the day.

If your plant leaves curl up, and your plant looks unhappy, take a close look under the leaves. If you do find aphids, there are a few simple ways to control their population, in addition to introducing beneficial insects and companion planting. The first step is to get a cloth and wipe them off. Even a quick blast of water from a sprayer will help dislodge them. Additionally, you can use a neem oil spray or insecticidal soap to knock down their numbers and discourage them from coming back.

However, any insecticide that will kill aphids will also kill off the beneficial bugs you have worked so hard to attract, so use them only as a last resort.

## *Spider Mites*

The next most common pest you will run into are spider mites. Unless you still have the eyesight of a teenager, it is unlikely you will be able to see these very small creatures, but you will not be able miss the fine webs that will cover your plants.

If you see spider mite webs, get out the neem oil and the insecticidal soaps. Also check your watering schedule, as they prefer dry soil. You might be able to slow down their return with damper soil and a persistent stubborn use of neem oil.

### Leaf Miners

When you are enjoying your afternoon beverage, and lazing about in your garden you can justify your relaxation by looking for leaf miners. These are more in the category of annoying insects than garden pest, but they share the same love of damaging your plants.

These show up as white insect trails on the leaf. If you press the trails between your fingers, you will often feel the insect move. You may also come across eggs, larvae, or even the insects themselves still inside the leaf.

If you see leaf miner damage, snip off the affected leaf and toss it away. Don't put these cuttings in your compost as the insects will walk or fly away in search of your other plants. Put them in the garbage so they are taken away to become residents of the local landfill.

### Cutworms

The final common pest we are going to talk about is the cutworm. These are the larval stage of moths that live on the underside of leaves. Instead of burrowing into the leaves, cutworms simply eat everything they can find. Think of them as that starving teenager that will eat the entire contents of your fridge and still look for more. Cutworms will eat the leaves, stems, and even the stalks of your plants, so if you come across them, you really need to remove them.

The most effective way is to pick them off and get rid of them. You can apply the neem oil and insecticidal soap to get rid of any that you missed

### The Rest of Them

I can hear the objections before you say them, so let me address the elephant in the room. What about, "insert insect name here?" Well, you will be pleased to know that the neem oil and insecticidal soap you are using on the aphids, spider mites, leaf miners, and cutworms will also discourage the rest of the common problematic insects.

If you are treating your plants for one type of insect, you are treating them for all the rest at the same time. I know there will always be some insects that may get past the neem oil and the insecticidal soap, but this is where the experts at your local garden supply store or nursery will come to the rescue.

You can be confident that whatever insect has decided to cause your problems will have been seen by others in your local area. Take this as an opportunity to connect with your local gardening groups and learn from them. So, pick their minds and together you will be able to determine how to control or eradicate all that is bothersome. Well, only insofar as insects, that is.

# Birds

Birds present a different type of problem. Typically, they will leave most vegetable gardens alone, as there is usually little of any interest to them. However, if you find they are going after your strawberries as they ripen, or you spot a jay helping itself to your peas, you must do something to keep them away.

If you have a strawberry patch, you can rig up some posts and string a net that covers the plants. Make sure the net reaches the ground at every spot. If there is an uncovered area, the birds might be able to get inside but not get out. Not only will this cause significant damage to your plants as the bird panics, but you could also harm the bird, and might be breaking local laws regarding the treatment of wild animals.

If you are not keen on using a net, you could hang shiny tape that will flutter in the wind, and supposedly scare away the birds, though I have experienced little success with this approach myself. Other options include fake hawks and other birds of prey that the small birds are afraid of. These can be as simple as a plastic hawk on a post to an animatronic model that moves and makes noise.

You could install an air cannon to randomly fire an explosion and scare the birds away, but there is a good chance that you will attract the police and that might put a damper on any further gardening.

Finally, you can head to your favorite thrift store and find all the clothes and accessories to resurrect a traditional scarecrow. Make it life sized and move it about every time you are in the garden. The theory goes that the birds will associate it with you and keep away.

Regardless of how you plan to deter the birds, make sure they are in fact a problem first, as some nice birdsong goes a long way to make the summer enjoyable.

# Others

This just leaves the rest. The cats, dogs, raccoons, badgers, possums, kangaroos, deer, moose, scorpions, hedgehogs, and whatever your local specialty is when it comes to small pests. Well, maybe we don't need to worry about the hedgehogs, but every different place will have their own flavor of annoying creatures.

So, what can be done about them?

The first step is to make sure you are not leaving out anything that might be considered food, other than your plants of course. This is one of the reasons to avoid putting dairy or meat in your compost. I have watched city raccoons open containers that I struggled with, so do your best to not give them any reason to investigate your compost. Yes, you could padlock them shut if your compost is in a container that can be locked, but that seems a bit extreme.

The lesson here is to keep your garden area clean. Clean of anything that could be food, clean of areas where these small wild animals can hide, and clean so that you can easily spot four-footed intruders.

Most of these pest creatures can be readily scared away by loud noises and movement, but when you start to run into cats, dogs, raccoons, and other much smarter creatures, you need to make sure they fear your yard and not you. If the garden remains appealing and they are only afraid of you, unless you set up a camp, they will still roam through your garden. Just not when you are around.

Ideally, your backyard will be so unpleasant for these animals they will never want to come back, and if they do there is one more unpleasant surprise for them, you.

That all sounds good but how do you achieve it? Unless you are trying to keep out deer, and most urban locations do not have wandering deer herds, there is little gained by fences. We've all seen cats and raccoons climb up and over vertical walls that would be hard to scale with a ladder. However, if you have problems with a dog, a fence might work well. But before you go to the cost and effort of fencing your garden, there are a few other options that might be worth investigating first.

A popular deterrent is the motion-activated sprinkler head. Run on batteries, these sprinkler heads are attached to your garden hose, with the pressure on and aimed where the pests have been seen. When they wander past the sensor, the sprinkler is activated for a set amount of time, then shuts off. As you are not present, there is no association between you and the water, so the garden becomes the hazard.

If you move the sprinkler head around your yard, it can act as an effective deterrent. The only real drawback is that you will be watering random sections of your yard. This extra water might disrupt or alter how your lawn and the rest of your non-vegetable plants grow.

A more significant consideration with these devices is the water use. As water bans and use restrictions become more and more common, the indiscriminate use of water to scare away pests might land you in hot water with the local bylaw enforcement officers.

You can also go old-school and build a scarecrow to randomly place around your yard. Now, the animal pests will be hesitant initially to come by with the zombie's new inhabitant in your backyard, but they will soon overcome their shyness and return. To keep them away long enough that they find another more attractive garden to bother, you can install several of the motion-activated noise makers now on the market.

By moving your scarecrow and the motion-activated noise makers about randomly, you should be able to make your garden unappealing. As with the sprinkler heads, you need to consider your neighbors when you set up the noise makers. It might not be worth the expense and effort to ring your backyard with them if they result in a noise complaint and a disturbing the peace ticket. I will leave it up to you to find the balance, but even if you only use the water and the noise devices in the day time, they will help to keep the pests away.

There are a few other tricks you can deploy while you wait for your main defenses to start to work, or if you have only a couple small pests to deal with. When it comes to cats, they are typically more interested in using your soil as a toilet than any of the plants, unless you grow catnip that is. If you have put down a couple inches of mulch around your plants, then at least the cats are less likely to dig up the soil, but odds are good they will still manage to spoil your garden. To stop this, I have found that a layer of mesh is all that is required.

You can use chicken wire, snow fencing, plastic mesh, or pretty much anything that catches your eye. All you need to do is cover the mulch. Make sure that you pin down the net or mesh with tent pegs or something similar so the cats cannot drag it aside. After a few days, the cats will have moved to some other garden they can dig up. Unfortunately, you will need to keep the mesh or net in place as cats are creatures of habit and will return now and again.

The net or mesh will also help prevent other creatures from digging in your soil. If they happen to fancy what you are growing, you might need to get a bit more creative. If you can find some tall bamboo stakes, plastic road edge markers, or even a section of pipe, you can put them in the ground at the corners of your garden and string a net over everything.

# Chapter 19: Harvest Time

*"It is like the seed put in the soil - the more one sows, the greater the harvest."*
— Orison Swett Marden

So here we are. The reason behind all that effort and time spent in the yard. Harvest. This can be extremely gratifying, as you now see the direct result of all your work for the last many months.

I am sure you have been watching all your fruit and vegetables grow and ripen over the last month with great expectations of harvest time. So, where do you start?

Now, before you get all carried away and start cutting everything down and bringing it inside, there are a couple considerations you would be well-served to ponder as you finish your drink.

The first thing to consider is how much produce you must deal with. Harvesting a basket of basil is a significantly different undertaking than having to deal with several 50-gallon bins full of produce. Do you have all the equipment ready? Do you know how you are going to manage each product? How long will that take? Will you need help?

Let's break it down into manageable bits so you don't get yourself into trouble and waste your harvest.

How are you going to deal with your harvest? This is a fundamental question because the answer will dictate how you proceed. Depending on the product, you might simply blanche and freeze your harvest as it comes inside. Blanching could be the ideal way to manage all your peas. Simply shell them and put them in boiling water for a few minutes. This will partially cook them and help keep them green once they are frozen. Put them in freezer bags or other freezer-safe containers.

If you are going to dry your harvest, you will need to know the capacity of your dehydrator. If you overfill it, the dehydrator will not be able to dry the produce before it starts to spoil.

So, knowing how much you can dry in each batch, how long that batch takes to finish, and you will know how much to harvest each day.

When it comes to making pickles, the volume that you can manage each day depends more on your processing facilities. If you are simply making fridge pickles, all you need to do is make the brine, clean the jars, put your produce in the jar and store in the fridge. They can then be in the fridge for a few weeks before they start to spoil and will either need to be eaten or disposed of then.

If you are planning to make sealed, shelf stable pickles then you will need either a pressure canner or a water bath canner. For now, you need to know that both canning methods will have a lengthy cooking/processing time that limits how much you can process over the course of a day.

The other approach to canning your harvest is to make it into the final product, the pasta sauce, chili, juice, or other products and then process into the shelf stable jars. This method requires more work at harvest time, but obviously, the work is done when you open the jar and want to eat it.

By making your harvest into the final form, you might find you use fewer canning jars, as juices, soups, and stews tend to reduce and concentrate your ingredients. This results in less work when you get to open the final product.

As you can see, it will depend greatly on both what you are harvesting and how you plan to process it as to how much you can pick each day. The exception to such a moderate pace is a frost warning.

A simple frost can not only damage the plants, but it can also have a significant impact on the produce you are about to harvest. If there is a frost in the forecast, you need to find all the boxes and containers that you can and bring everything inside, except for parsnips. Parsnips become much sweeter if they are subjected to frost and then harvested.

If you do end up with rooms full of harvested produce due to the weather not cooperating, you will need to process it or store it as soon as you can lest it spoils. If you have green tomatoes, they will eventually ripen, so you can focus your time on the rest of your produce and get back to them later.

# When Is It Ready?

That all sounds good and makes sense, but how do you know when things are ready for harvest? Again, I must use that annoying answer, it depends.

When you planted your seeds, you recorded the approximate harvest date on your phone. So, you can now reference that information and see how close you are. Keep in mind that the harvest date on the seed packages can be both optimistic and pessimistic. The ripening time of the plant may have been determined in a lab environment and your garden location might mean your plants are faster or slower to mature.

When you are considering when is the right time to harvest the produce, there are a couple surefire methods that will ensure you pick the produce at the perfect time.

The first approach will require the help of an experienced gardener friend. Bribe them with the promise of amazing produce, or a beverage of their preference, and have them take a stroll through your garden.

The subtle signs and indications your produce is ready to harvest can be hard to spot when you are new to gardening, but after a couple years the significance of a dry stem or stretched tight skin will alert you to get your snips ready.

If you do not have a friend that gardens, or the correct bribe to bring them by, then what do you do? Conveniently, all you need to do is to fall back on your old patterns.

What I mean by that is to head down to your local grocery store and have a real close look at the produce. Yes, the produce at the grocery store is not always the best example, but it will serve as a very real example as to fruit and vegetables that are ripe enough to eat.

Of course, your produce will look much better than what you can find at the store, but if we look at the tomatoes for a moment, you will see that while they are all likely red, some will be much harder than others, their stems will vary from soft and flexible to dried and brittle. The skin will range from smooth and shiny to wrinkled and dull. Now, here is the real reason you headed back to the grocery store.

The produce manager. Make a point to find this person and ask them how you know when your tomatoes, strawberries, or whichever fruit or vegetable you are looking at is ready to harvest. They will be able to give you a great deal of specific information on what to look for. Now, not only will you learn that a dull skin on a tomato means it has already gone beyond the perfect ripeness, but you can also hold one in your hands to fully appreciate what those words really mean. The same with carrots, potatoes, and all the other produce in your garden.

There is some value in me telling you that spaghetti squash is ready to harvest when their skin is hard, and they sound hollow when you tap on them. But there is great value in that sentence when you have a spaghetti squash in your hands, can feel the hard skin, and hear the hollowness. When you can combine the words with an example, you will never forget what to look for.

Keep in mind most produce managers are very busy people, but if you show interest in their expertise, I have found that most people are willing to make time to teach you what they themselves love about fresh produce.

The last option, and really it can be very hit and miss, is to simply pick something from your garden, eat it, and can tolerate the taste then you can call it ripe and ready to harvest. I am not a big fan of this method, but if there is no other way that you can determine if your produce is ready to harvest, then try it. But keep in mind a great deal of the fruits and vegetables that you are growing will taste wonderful when ripe and unpalatable when not.

## How Much to Take

As we have already mentioned, the most significant impact on your harvest will be where you live and where you are in the growing cycle. Mid-July might see you only harvest enough for your daily needs, while late in the fall might find you pulling out entire plants before the first killing frost puts an end to your gardening plans for the year. Obviously, if you live somewhere warm you might be able to grow two or more full crops during a year, in which case you might be pulling out your plants to replace them with new seedlings and start the entire cycle again.

So, there you stand in front of your garden with your snips in one hand and your beautiful vintage harvest basket in the other. What is the next step? Do you cut everything off at the ground, drag it all inside and then figure out what to do with it? Do you just cut off the leaves? What about the stems, the stalks, and flowers if there are any left?

Again, I am going to have to use that horrendous excuse for an answer. It depends. Yeah, I know, but hold on a sec, and let me explain, because there is logic behind that answer.

Let's start with tomatoes. The only part of the plant you ever see at the grocery store is that short section of vine holding the tomatoes together for the "grown on the vine" variety of tomatoes. All the rest of the tomatoes are stemless. So, unless you want tomatoes on the vine, you can just carefully pluck the ripe tomatoes off the stem.

This is true for peppers, cucumbers, peas, beans, you get the idea. If you have seen the produce at the grocery store with a stem, then harvest the stem. If the stem is missing, then you don't need to harvest it. You can be assured that the people behind shipping all the produce to your local grocery store are only willing to pay for what needs to accompany the produce and not more than that.

This approach does get a bit misleading for celery, as you are unlikely to see celery in the produce section of your grocery store with leaves still attached. But not only are they safe to eat, they have a wonderful light taste. So, keep them on the celery and you will not be disappointed.

The opposite is true for rhubarb. The stems are tasty, but the leaves are poisonous. So, when you harvest rhubarb, gently pull the stalk off the parent plant, and make sure to cut away all the leaf material.

I know you want me to give a few guidelines to know when you harvest the garden. Here they are, but please keep in mind that your variety might become harvest-ready and show different signs than those I will list here.

You can harvest herbs once the leaves are large enough for you. Try not to harvest everything from one plant or stalk but spread it out over all your plants to have the least impact on each individual plant so they will continue to grow.

Peas, beans, tomatoes, cucumbers, peppers and many other fruits and vegetables are ready to harvest when they are the color you expect. For example, your tomatoes are ready if you are growing a red variety and the skin feels plump and soft to the touch. Most fruit and vegetables will change color first, then their skin will soften as they ripen.

Carrots, radishes, beets, and other root vegetables will usually start to push up through the soil as they ripen. Once you see a good-sized shoulder sticking up, you can pull one and see how close to ready it is.

Potatoes, sweet potatoes, and other ground tubers will usually be ripe once the above ground portion of the plant has flowered and started to die back. Ideally, other than parsnips, you should pull the plants and harvest the tubers before the killing frost if for no other reason than the frost will kill the plants and make them slimy and slippery to handle.

This should give you some simple guidelines for that first harvest. Quite quickly you will learn when your plants are ready to be harvested every year thereafter. Keep trying, keep learning. Don't overlook the value of learning experience.

# Chapter 20: Seed Harvesting

*"It's incredible to reflect on how much knowledge and growth power is contained in seeds."*
— Charles Dowding

The other aspect of harvesting is collecting seeds you will need for next year. All you need is a couple plants of each of the varieties you have grown and left to flower and go to seed.

Now, you do not have to worry so much about this for your tomato, peppers, squash, beans, or peas. The seeds can be harvested from your food harvest.

But when it comes to herbs, lettuce, carrots, onions, and others you will need to have plants that have not been harvested for food. These plants will add a great splash of color in your garden, along with providing you with seeds for next year.

The specific details on each plant will be covered in their growing guide, but you do need to understand the big picture view of the entire process before you begin.

We have already covered the importance of heirloom and open-pollinated plants, as they will produce seeds that will be very similar to the parent plant you harvested them from. The seeds from any hybrid plant can be collected, stored, and re-used next year, but there is no guarantee that the plants that grow will be the same as the parent plant. If you are interested in plant husbandry, planting the seeds from hybrids might be the perfect source of interesting and new varieties.

But most people want to regrow the same plants they grew the previous year. To make sure you have viable seeds for the next spring, there are a few key pointers.

The idea behind seed harvest and storage is to delay the onset of germination until you are ready for it to happen. The simple solution is to remove all the triggers from the seed, such as water and light in most cases. Once the seeds have been removed from their germination triggers, they need to be kept in a stable environment.

The most common reason for seed storage failure is the introduction of moisture. Even the smallest amount of moisture can trigger germination or provide the perfect environment for mold. Either of these will destroy your seeds.

## Preparation

The first step in storing seeds is to separate them from their surrounding media. Depending on the plant, this could be the pulp of a tomato, the insides of your pumpkin, or as simple as shaking all the seeds of the plant into a container.

With all the seeds collected, you need to remove all the debris that was also collected, so you will end up with only the seeds to be put into storage.

## Storage

Once you have isolated the seeds, you can put them into storage. Now, we are not going to try and replicate the perfect storage conditions that you would see in a seed bank. We just want to create the conditions for your seeds to last the winter and still be viable come spring.

Small envelopes can be the perfect storage solution, as you can write on each one the details of the seeds, and you can store all your seeds in a single larger container. I recommend this approach as it will keep your seeds very well organized. Add a few of those silica desiccant packages in the larger container to keep the moisture level below the trigger point of 40 percent relative humidity.

In addition to keeping all your seeds in a dry environment, you also need to do your best to keep them cool. The ideal storage location is kept between 2 and 4 degrees Celsius, (35 to 40F). This will ensure that your seeds will last as long as possible.

# Labeling

Now, I know we all think that we have great memories, and that actually putting a label on each of your seeds packages is nothing more than a waste of time. Let me do my best to convince you otherwise unless of course you like the surprise you will get next summer when you plant the unlabeled seeds.

If you are like the majority of us, you like to know what you are planting. As you remember from the chapter on companion planting, it can have a significant impact on your garden if you try to grow the wrong plants beside each other.

To remove the possibility of growing your peas, carrots, and leeks all in the same small pot as your basil, label the seeds that you collect in the fall.

In a perfect world, you would label each small seed envelope with the name of the plant. I am hoping your label is as simple as basil, red peppers, cucumbers. Keep it simple. If you feel the need to add your pet's name, then go right ahead, as you have obviously formed a deep connection with the plant and you will be more inclined to look after it well.

After the name, include the harvest date and year so you can compare how the seeds preform from one year to the next, as well as track how old your seeds are. This will give you an idea of how long your seed preservation techniques last, and thus the life expectancy of the rest of your seed collection.

If you feel inclined, and still have the space on the envelope, add where the parent plant came from. Was it a store-bought seedling, commercial seeds, or one of your collected seeds?

Why should you bother with all this extra information? As you develop your gardening skills, you might focus on productivity, or aesthetics, or some other aspect of your plants, and knowing where your plants came from will allow you to source more seeds you need them.

Part of that record is the seeds that you grew and the seeds that you harvested. You might have a situation where you were able to harvest an incredible crop one year but the seeds from those plants were duds the next. If you recorded the details of the seeds and the associated plants, you would know to dispose of the low-yield seeds and find or purchase others that will give you a better harvest.

Year-by-year records also give you a very good indication of the specifics of your local climate. After the third or fourth year, you have a good idea when the frost leaves in the spring and when it returns in the fall.

You can use this information to determine what plants you need to start inside, when they need to be germinated by, and which plants you can plant outside as seeds.

There is one last advantage to recording as much information as you can during the season. This is a reason that I have not seen mentioned before, but I know it has helped me over the last few years, so I figured it was worth passing along.

Winter boredom.

Yep. There you sit, the snow is on the ground, and you cannot grow anything. So, what can you do besides binge-watch your favorite streaming show? Well, you can dream about the coming summer and plan your garden.

You see? You have all the information that you could ever ask for at your fingertips, provided of course you recorded it last year.

You can look at the garden plans, your harvest numbers, the seeds that you used, how much fertilizer and water you used and look at what worked and what didn't. Grab those notes, your tablet if you are tech savvy, or a pad of paper.

Now the fun part is figuring out how to make next year's garden even better. Does that mean more flowers? More herbs? More squash? I cannot tell you, only you know that, but what is better than a day spent dreaming about the coming summer and all that great time you'll have in your garden?

# Chapter 21: Year End

*"The garden year has no beginning and no end."*

- Elizabeth Lawrence

Here we are at the end of the season. You have all your produce harvested and either stored away for the winter or in process of being stored. I am sure you have looked at your garden area and wondered what you need to do before the winter sets in.

There are several different approaches to dealing with your garden over the winter. None of them are the "correct" way as each has benefits and drawbacks. You will need to decide which approach is the most suited to your garden, and both your temperament, and aesthetics.

As you might expect, the simplest approach is to do nothing. Once you have harvested your produce, you simply pull out your plants and toss them in the compost. You turn your back on your soil and don't give any of it a second thought until spring.

This will greatly reduce your workload in the fall but increase the amount of spring work. With your soil resting over the winter, you will need to add fertilizer or compost as soon as you are able to work the soil in the spring. This will give as much time as possible for your soil to stabilize and adjust to the new nutrient levels before you transplant in your seedlings or plant your seeds.

If you are pressed for time in the fall and feel you can make up the lost work in the spring, then this might be for you.

The next approach is to add your fertilizer or compost in the fall, once you have pulled out all your plants that will not survive the winter. This will make sure the fertilizer and compost will have plenty of time to incorporate into the soil. With this method, you can plant your seeds and transplant your seedlings a few weeks earlier than with the first method, as there is no risk of the high levels of nutrients in the compost or fertilizer burning the plants.

This will give you the additional time you need to grow some of the longer-season plants, without needing to start them inside.

The final approach to dealing with your soil over the winter is a combination of the two mentioned methods. Remove all the plants that will not survive the winter and add your fertilizer and compost. This allows it to mellow and incorporate into the soil over the winter. When you are ready to start the garden again in the spring, you do a soil test and add the required fertilizer to bring the soil nutrient levels up to the optimum levels for the plants you want to grow.

The first two methods provide good soil for your plants in the next growing season, but the third method is more likely to provide the ideal level of nutrients to enable your plants to thrive.

These three approaches will, at a minimum, make sure that all the time, money, and effort that you have put into your soil will still pay dividends the next season.

The overarching philosophy behind your garden is to have a garden space that works for you. The location, soil, sun exposure, and what you grow will impact how you manage the soil when you are not growing plants.

Once you have a season or two under your gardening belt, you will know what techniques and methods work best for you.

A final note on post-harvest work. When you have harvested all your produce and pulled out the dead plants, make sure to clean all your tools before you put them away for the winter.

If there are any diseases, soil dwelling insects, or other problems, they are likely to be transferred to your shovel, hoe, and trowels during the growing season. To ensure these problems are not re-introduced to your soil the next year, hose down your tools.

Wash away all the accumulated dirt and muck and let your tools air dry in the sunshine. Once they are clean and dry, store them for the winter and know that when you need them in the spring, they will be clean and ready to use.

# Chapter 22: Common Mistakes and Solutions

*"There are no gardening mistakes, only experiments."*

— Janet Kilburn Phillips

As with everything we as humans learn, we make mistakes. I know this list is accurate because I did them all as I learned to garden.

1. Planting mint in beds and not containers.
    a. Mint is a very aggressive spreading plant that can rapidly take over your garden plot. Once established, it is very difficult to remove. You will need to replace all the soil in your garden to make sure the mint is gone as a single section of root can regrow into an aggressive new mint plant.

2. Not spacing your plants properly.
    a. If you are anything like me, you will want to plant more plants than your garden can accommodate. You need to have the space between all your plants to allow them to grow and produce their crops. So, take a breath, give your plants the space. Let them grow with the spacing detailed in the growing guides or on the seed packages.

3. Not using mulch.
    a. As you know, by not using mulch you allow weeds to establish, your soil to heat too much, and potentially dry out faster than you are able to keep it watered.

4. Not enough light.
    a. Keep your eyes open to where you have sunlight and where you do not. Make sure that you plant the correct type of plant in each area to take advantage of the different light levels.

5. Stopping too soon.
    a. Your first year of gardening will have its ups and downs. Don't let this stop you. Even if you don't manage to grow a single thing the first year, know that it can only get better next year.

6. And the rest.
    a. Anyone with any gardening experience will have a similar list of lessons learned. When you have yours, share these with new gardeners. Save them so much doubt and anxiety. It can only help to know that we all go through the same learning steps and missteps as we become gardeners. Keep in mind that it will be better next year, or the next, or the next. Becoming a gardener will bring out your optimism.

# Chapter 23: Growing Guides

*"Gardeners, I think, dream bigger dreams than emperors."*

– Mary Cantwell

With every plant needing slightly different amounts of watering, nutrients, and light to grow to its ideal size and productivity, I have included a growing guide for each of the plants that we identified in Chapter 4.

Once you have a good harvest or two under your belt, you will be ready to branch out and select less common plants and you will have the skills you need to keep them alive until harvest.

The details listed in the individual growing guides are based on commercial production requirements. These have been independently tested to not only keep the plants healthy throughout the growing season but provide the most abundant yields with the least input and work.

Not all the plants listed will be suitable for all hardiness zones, but depending on your local microclimate you should be able to grow most of them. If you like the idea of growing any or all the plants listed, I would encourage you to try. While you may not produce the largest harvest in the fall, I am confident that you will learn about that plant and have a much better idea what is required to grow it next year.

I have left these guides until the end of the book, so they are readily accessible as reference during the growing season.

# Summary of Information for Common Vegetable Garden Plants

|  | **Asparagus** | **Basil** | **Beans** | **Beets** | **Broccoli** |
|---|---|---|---|---|---|
| Soil pH | 6.5-7.5 | 5.5-6.5 | 6-7 | 6-7 | 6-7 |
| Germination Time (days) | 21-28 | 5-10 | 7-14 | 7-14 | 7-14 |
| Indoor start weeks before last frost | 6-8 | 4-6 | 2 | 2 | 6-8 |
| Ideal Soil Depth (in/mm) | 12/300 | 1/25 | 1-2/25-50 | 1-2/25-50 | 1/25 |
| Seed Spacing (in/mm) | 6/150 | 8/200 | 2-4/50-100 | 2/50 | 4-6/100-150 |
| Seed Planting Depth (in/mm) | 1-2/25-50 | 1/25 | 1-2/25-50 | 1/25 | 0.25-0.5/6-13 |
| Seedling Spacing (in/mm) | 12/300 | 8/200 | 6-8/150-200 | 3-4/75-100 | 18/450 |
| Seedling Planting Depth (in/mm) | 6/150 | 1/25 | 1-2/25-50 | 1/25 | 0.25-0.5/6-13 |
| Min Soil Temp (°C/°F) | 10/50 | 18/65 | 16/60 | 10/50 | 10/50 |
| Row Spacing (in/mm) | 18-24/450-600 | 12/300 | 18-24/450-600 | 12/300 | 18-24/450-600 |
| Time Until Harvest (days) | 365-730 | 60-90 | 50-80 | 50-70 | 50-100 |

|  | **Brussels Sprouts** | **Cabbage** | **Carrots** | **Cauliflower** | **Celery** |
|---|---|---|---|---|---|
| Soil pH | 6-7 | 6.5-7.5 | 6.0-6.8 | 6.0-7.0 | 6.0-6.8 |
| Germination Time (days) | 7-14 | 7-10 | 10-14 | 7-10 | 10-14 |
| Indoor Start (weeks) | 10-12 | 4-6 | 2-4 | 4-6 | 10-12 |
| Ideal Soil Depth (in/mm) | 1/25 | 12-18/ 305-457 | 12-18/ 305-457 | 12-18 / 305-457 | 12-18/ 305-457 |
| Seed Spacing (in/mm) | 4-6/100-150 | 2 / 50 | 2 / 50 | 2 / 50 | 2 / 50 |
| Seed Planting Depth (in/mm) | 0.25-0.5/6-13 | 0.5 / 13 | 0.25 / 6 | 0.5 / 13 | 0.125 / 3 |
| Seedling Spacing (in/mm) | 18/450 | 18 / 457 | 3-4 / 76-102 | 18 / 457 | 8-10/ 203-254 |
| Seedling Planting Depth (in/mm) | 0.25-0.5/6-13 | 0.5-1 / 13-25 | 0.25-0.5 / 6-13 | 0.5-1 / 13-25 | 0.125-0.25 / 3-6 |
| Min Soil Temp (°C/°F) | 10/50 | 10/50 | 10/50 | 10/50 | 15/ 60 |
| Row Spacing (in/mm) | 24/60 | 24 / 610 | 12 / 305 | 24 / 610 | 24 / 610 |
| Time Until Harvest (days) | 85-120 | 60-180 | 70-80 | 50-100 | 120 |

| | **Collard Greens** | **Cucumber** | **Dill** | **Eggplant** | **Garlic** |
|---|---|---|---|---|---|
| Soil pH | 6.0-7.5 | 6.0-7.0 | 5.5-6.5 | 5.5-6.8 | 6.0-7.0 |
| Germination Time (days) | 4-12 | 7-14 | 7-14 | 7-14 | 7-14 |
| Indoor Start (weeks) | 6-8 | 2-4 | - | 6-8 | - |
| Ideal Soil Depth (in/mm) | 18-24/45-60 | 12-18/30-45 | 12/30 | 12-18/30-45 | 4/10 |
| Seed Spacing (in/mm) | 2-4/5-10 | 4-6/10-15 | 2-3/5-7.5 | 18-24/45-60 | 4-6/10-15 |
| Seed Planting Depth (in/mm) | 0.5-1/13-25 | 1-1.5/25-38 | 0.25-0.5/6-13 | 0.5-1/13-25 | 2/51 |
| Seedling Spacing (in/mm) | 12-18/30-45 | 24-36/60-90 | 6/15 | 24-36/60-90 | 4-6/10-15 |
| Seedling Planting Depth (in/mm) | 0.5-1/13-25 | 1-1.5/25-38 | 0.25/6 | 0.5-1/13-25 | 2/51 |
| Min Soil Temp (°C/°F) | 10/50 | 18/65 | 15/60 | 21/70 | 10/50 |
| Row Spacing (in/mm) | 24-30/60-75 | 36-48/90-120 | 18/45 | 36-48/90-120 | 18/45 |
| Time Until Harvest (days) | 50-75 | 50-70 | 80-90 | 65-85 | 90-150 |

|  | Kale | Leek | Lettuce | Melons | Onions |
|---|---|---|---|---|---|
| Soil pH | 6.0-7.5 | 6.0-7.0 | 6.0-7.0 | 6.0-7.5 | 6.0-7.5 |
| Germination Time (days) | 5-10 | 10-14 | 7-14 | 5-10 | 10-14 |
| Indoor Start (weeks) | 4-6 | 12-14 | 4-6 | 2-4 | 10-12 |
| Ideal Soil Depth (in/mm) | 6/150 | 6/150 | 6/150 | 12/300 | 6/150 |
| Seed Spacing (in/mm) | 1-2/25-50 | 2/50 | 1/25 | 3-4/75-100 | 2/50 |
| Seed Planting Depth (in/mm) | 0.5/13 | 0.5-1/13-25 | 0.25/6.4 | 1/25.4 | 0.5/13 |
| Seedling Spacing (in/mm) | 18-24/450-600 | 6/150 | 8-12/200-300 | 36/900 | 6/150 |
| Seedling Planting Depth (in/mm) | 0.5/13 | 6/150 | 0.25/6.4 | 1/25 | 0.5/13 |
| Min Soil Temp (°C/°F) | 7/45 | 10/50 | 10/50 | 21/70 | 7/45 |
| Row Spacing (in/mm) | 18/450 | 18/450 | 12/300 | 60/1500 | 12/300 |
| Time Until Harvest (days) | 55-75 | 90-120 | 40-75 | 80-100 | 100-120 |

|  | **Okra** | **Parsley** | **Parsnips** | **Peas** | **Peppers** |
|---|---|---|---|---|---|
| Soil pH | 6.0-7.0 | 6.0-7.0 | 5.5-7.5 | 6.0-7.5 | 6.0-6.8 |
| Germination Time (days) | 7-14 | 14-21 | 14-21 | 7-14 | 7-14 |
| Indoor Start (weeks) | 2-4 | 8-10 | 4-6 | 4-6 | 6-8 |
| Ideal Soil Depth (in/mm) | 12/300 | 6/150 | 12/300 | 2/50 | 12/300 |
| Seed Spacing (in/mm) | 6/150 | 1/25 | 2-3/50-75 | 2-3/50-75 | 2-3/50-75 |
| Seed Planting Depth (in/mm) | 1/25.4 | 1/25 | 0.5-1/13-25 | 1-2/25-50 | 0.25/6 |
| Seedling Spacing (in/mm) | 18-24/450-600 | 6/150 | 3-4/75-100 | 2-4/50-100 | 18/450 |
| Seedling Planting Depth (in/mm) | 1/25.4 | 1/25 | 0.5-1/13-25 | 1-2/25-50 | 6/150 |
| Min Soil Temp (°C/°F) | 18/65 | 10/50 | 7/45 | 10/50 | 18/65 |
| Row Spacing (in/mm) | 36/90 | 12/300 | 18/450 | 24/600 | 18/450 |
| Time Until Harvest (days) | 50-65 | 70-90 | 100-130 | 50-70 | 70-85 |

|  | **Potatoes** | **Pumpkins** | **Radish** | **Raspberries** | **Rhubarb** |
|---|---|---|---|---|---|
| Soil pH | 5.5-6.5 | 5.5-6.8 | 5.5-6.5 | 6.0-6.5 | 5.5-6.8 |
| Germination Time (days) | 14-28 | 6-10 | 3-5 | 10-14 | 14-21 |
| Indoor Start (weeks) | 4-6 | 3-4 | - | - | - |
| Ideal Soil Depth (in/mm) | 12/300 | 12 in. | 1-2 in. | - | - |
| Seed Spacing (in/mm) | 12/300 | 4-6/10-15 | 1 in. | - | - |
| Seed Planting Depth (in/mm) | 4-6/100-150 | 1 in. | 1/2 in. | - | 1-2 in. |
| Seedling Spacing (in/mm) | 12/300 | 3-4 ft. | 2-3 in. | - | 3-4 ft. |
| Seedling Planting Depth (in/mm) | 2-4/50-10 | 1/25 | 1/2 in. | - | 1/25 |
| Min Soil Temp (°C/°F) | 15/60 | 15/60 | 10/50 | 10/50 | 7/45 |
| Row Spacing (in/mm) | 2-3 ft | 5-6 ft. | 6-18 in. | - | 3-4 ft. |
| Time Until Harvest (days) | 90-120 | 75-120 | 21-60 | 2-3 years | 1-2 years |

| | **Turnips** | **Spinach** | **Squash** | **Strawberries** | **Sweet Corn** |
|---|---|---|---|---|---|
| Soil pH | 6.0-6.8 | 6.0-7.5 | 5.5-7.5 | 5.5-7.0 | 5.8-7.0 |
| Germination Time (days) | 5-10 | 7-14 | 7-14 | 14-21 | 7-10 |
| Indoor Start (weeks) | - | 6-8 weeks | 2-3 weeks | N/A | 2 weeks |
| Ideal Soil Depth (in/mm) | 1/4-1/2 in. | 1/2 in (13 mm) | 18 in (46 cm) | N/A | 6-12 in (15-30 cm) |
| Seed Spacing (in/mm) | 2-4 in. | 1 in (25 mm) | 4-6 seeds per hill | 12-18 in (305-457 mm) | 8-12 in (20-30 cm) |
| Seed Planting Depth (in/mm) | 1/4-1/2 in. | 1/2 in (13 mm) | 1-2 in (25-51 mm) | Surface Sow | 1-2 in (25-51 mm) |
| Seedling Spacing (in/mm) | 4-6 in. apart | 3-6 in (76-152 mm) | 36-48 in (91-122 cm) | N/A | 24-30 in (61-76 cm) |
| Seedling Planting Depth (in/mm) | 1/4-1/2 in. | 1-2/ 25-51 | 1-2/ 25-51 | N/A | 1-2/ 25-51 |
| Min Soil Temp (°C/°F) | 10 / 50 | 7/45 | 18/65 | 10/50 | 16/60 |
| Row Spacing (in/mm) | 12-18 in. | 12-18 in (305-457 mm) | 4-6 ft (1.2-1.8 m) | 18-24 in (457-610 mm) | 30 in (762 mm) |
| Time Until Harvest (days) | 45-50 | 40-50 | 50-60 | 30-60 | 60-100 |

|  | **Sweet Potato** | **Swiss Chard** | **Tomato** | **Oregano** | **Zucchini** |
|---|---|---|---|---|---|
| Soil pH | 5.6-6.6 | 6-7.5 | 6-7 | 6-8 | 6-7 |
| Germination Time (days) | 7-14 | 5-7 | 6-10 | 10-14 | 4-7 |
| Indoor Start (weeks) | 6-8 weeks | 4-6 | 6-8 | 8-10 | 2-4 |
| Ideal Soil Depth (in/mm) | 6-8 in (15-20 cm) | 12-18" | 12-18" | - | 12-18" |
| Seed Spacing (in/mm) | 12-18/305-457 | 3-4 | 24-36 | - | 36-60 |
| Seed Planting Depth (in/mm) | 3-4 in (76-102 mm) | 1/2 | 1/4 | 1/4 | 1 |
| Seedling Spacing (in/mm) | 12-18 in (305-457 mm) | 6-10 | 24-36 | - | 36-60 |
| Seedling Planting Depth (in/mm) | 3-4/ 76-102 | 4-6 | 1-2/ 25-51 | - | 1-2/ 25-51 |
| Min Soil Temp (°C/°F) | 21°C/70°F | 10/50 | 15/60 | 15/60 | 15/60 |
| Row Spacing (in/mm) | 3-4 ft (0.9-1.2 m) | 12/30 | 24-36/60-90 | 12-18/30-45 | 36-60/90-150 |
| Time Until Harvest (days) | 90-17 | 50-60 | 70-90 | 85-90 | |

# Companion Planting

| Plant | Good Companion Plants | Bad Companion Plants |
|---|---|---|
| Asparagus | Tomatoes, parsley, basil, dill, marigolds | Garlic, onions |
| Basil | Tomatoes, peppers, oregano, asparagus, petunias | Rue, sage, cucumber |
| Beans | Carrots, celery, corn, cucumbers, beets | Onions, garlic, gladiolus, leek |
| Beets | Bush beans, onions, garlic | Pole beans |
| Broccoli | Basil, dill, chamomile, marigolds, nasturtiums, rosemary, sage | Tomatoes, strawberries, pole beans |
| Brussels Sprouts | Dill, chamomile, peppermint, rosemary, sage, thyme | Strawberries |
| Cabbage | Dill, chamomile, rosemary, sage, thyme, beets, celery | Strawberries, tomatoes, pole beans, celery |
| Carrots | Peas, onions, leeks, rosemary, sage, tomatoes | Dill, parsnips |
| Cauliflower | Nasturtiums, marigolds, thyme | Strawberries, tomatoes |
| Celery | Nasturtiums, onions, leeks | Cabbages |
| Collard Greens | Mint, chamomile, thyme | Tomatoes |
| Cucumber | Sunflowers, radishes, marigolds, nasturtiums | Aromatic herbs, potatoes |
| Dill | Cabbage, corn, lettuce, onions | Tomatoes, carrots, cucumber |
| Eggplant | Beans, marigolds, peas, peppers, spinach | Fennel |
| Garlic | Beets, chamomile, lettuce, strawberries | Beans, peas, asparagus |
| Kale | Dill, chamomile, mint, thyme | Strawberries |
| Leek | Carrots, celery, onions | Beans, peas |
| Lettuce | Carrots, radishes, strawberries | Parsley |
| Melons | Corn, pumpkins, radishes, marigolds, nasturtiums | Potatoes |
| Onions | Beets, strawberries, tomatoes, chamomile, summer savory | Beans, peas, asparagus |
| Okra | Eggplant, peppers | None reported |

| | | |
|---|---|---|
| Parsley | Asparagus, corn, tomatoes | Mint, cucumber, lettuce |
| Parsnips | Garlic, onions, peas | Carrots |
| Peas | Carrots, turnips, radishes, cucumbers | Onions, garlic, gladiolus, leek |
| Peppers | Basil, carrots, onions | Fennel |
| Potatoes | Beans, corn, marigolds, peas | Tomatoes, cucumber, melon, pumpkins, raspberries, squash, zucchini |
| Pumpkins | Corn, melons, radishes, marigolds, nasturtiums | Potatoes |
| Radish | Cucumbers, lettuce, peas, nasturtiums | Hyssop |
| Raspberries | Tansy | Potatoes |
| Rhubarb | Beans, cauliflower, peas | None reported |
| Turnips | Peas | None reported |
| Spinach | None reported | Strawberries |
| Squash | Corn, radishes, marigolds, nasturtiums | Potatoes |
| Strawberries | Borage, lettuce, spinach | Cabbages, broccoli, brussel sprouts, cauliflower, kale, spinach |
| Sweet Corn | Cucumbers, melons, peas, pumpkins, beans | Tomatoes |
| Sweet Potato | Beans, peas, spinach | Brassicas, fennel |
| Swiss Chard | Beans, peas, radish, onions | Brassicas, grapes, melons |
| Tomato | Basil, onions, parsley | Brassicas, fennel, broccoli, cabbage, Cauliflower, collard greens, dill, potatoes, sweet corn |
| Oregano | Broccoli, cabbage, grapes | Beans, peas, cucumber |
| Zucchini | Beans, corn, peas | Potatoes, fennel |

# Seed Harvest and Storage

|  | Harvesting Seeds | Storing Seeds |
|---|---|---|
| Asparagus | Allow the seed pods to dry and turn brown before harvesting. | Store in a cool, dry place in a labeled envelope or container. |
| Basil | Allow the plant to flower and the seeds to dry on the stalk. | Store in a cool, dry place in a labeled envelope or container. |
| Beans | Allow the pods to dry on the plant, then remove and shell the beans. | Store in a cool, dry place in a labeled envelope or container. |
| Beets | Allow the flowers to mature and develop seed heads, then harvest the seeds. | Store in a cool, dry place in a labeled envelope or container. |
| Broccoli | Allow the seed pods to dry and turn brown on the plant, then harvest the seeds. | Store in a cool, dry place in a labeled envelope or container. |
| Brussels Sprouts | Allow the seed pods to dry and turn brown on the plant, then harvest the seeds. | Store in a cool, dry place in a labeled envelope or container. |
| Cabbage | Allow the seed pods to dry and turn brown on the plant, then harvest the seeds. | Store in a cool, dry place in a labeled envelope or container. |
| Carrots | Allow the seed heads to dry on the plant, then harvest the seeds. | Store in a cool, dry place in a labeled envelope or container. |
| Cauliflower | Allow the seed pods to dry and turn brown on the plant, then harvest the seeds. | Store in a cool, dry place in a labeled envelope or container. |
| Celery | Allow the seed heads to dry on the plant, then harvest the seeds. | Store in a cool, dry place in a labeled envelope or container. |
| Collard Greens | Allow the plant to flower and the seeds to dry on the stalk. | Store in a cool, dry place in a labeled envelope or container. |
| Cucumber | Allow the cucumber to mature and turn yellow, then remove the seeds. | Rinse and dry the seeds, then store in a cool, dry place in a labeled envelope or container. |
| Dill | Allow the seed heads to dry on the plant, then harvest the seeds. | Store in a cool, dry place in a labeled envelope or container. |
| Eggplant | Allow the fruit to mature and turn yellow, then remove the seeds. | Rinse and dry the seeds, then store in a cool, dry place in a labeled envelope or container. |

| | | |
|---|---|---|
| Garlic | Allow the plant to flower and the seeds to dry on the stalk. | Store in a cool, dry place in a labeled envelope or container. |
| Kale | Allow the plant to flower and the seeds to dry on the stalk. | Store in a cool, dry place in a labeled envelope or container. |
| Leek | Allow the plant to flower and the seeds to dry on the stalk. | Store in a cool, dry place in a labeled envelope or container. |
| Lettuce | Allow the seed heads to dry on the plant, then harvest the seeds. | Store in a cool, dry place in a labeled envelope or container. |
| Melon | Allow the fruit to mature and turn yellow, then remove the seeds. | Rinse and dry the seeds, then store in a cool, dry place in a labeled envelope or container. |
| Onions | Allow the flowers to mature and develop seed heads, then harvest the seeds. | Store in a cool, dry place in a labeled envelope or container. |
| Okra | Allow the pods to mature and turn brown on the plant, then remove and dry them. | Store in a cool, dry place in a labeled envelope or container. |
| Parsley | Allow the seed heads to dry on the plant, then harvest the seeds. | Store in a cool, dry place in a labeled envelope or container. |
| Parsnips | Allow the flowers to mature and develop seed heads, then harvest the seeds. | Store in a cool, dry place in a labeled envelope or container. |
| Peas | Allow the pods to dry on the plant, then remove and shell the peas. | Store in a cool, dry place in a labeled envelope or container. |
| Peppers | Allow the peppers to mature and turn red or yellow, then remove the seeds. | Rinse and dry the seeds, then store in a cool, dry place in a labeled envelope or container. |
| Potatoes | Allow the seed balls to mature and turn brown on the plant, then harvest them. | Store in a cool, dry place in a labeled envelope or container. |
| Pumpkins | Allow the fruit to mature and turn brown, then remove and dry the seeds. | Store in a cool, dry place in a labeled envelope or container. |
| Radish | Allow the seed pods to dry and turn brown on the plant, then harvest the seeds. | Store in a cool, dry place in a labeled envelope or container. |
| Raspberries | Allow the fruit to mature and turn dark red, then remove and dry the seeds. | Store in a cool, dry place in a labeled envelope or container. |

| | | |
|---|---|---|
| Rhubarb | Allow the seed heads to dry on the plant, then harvest the seeds. | Store in a cool, dry place in a labeled envelope or container. |
| Turnips | Allow the seed pods to dry and turn brown on the plant, then harvest the seeds. | Store in a cool, dry place in a labeled envelope or container. |
| Spinach | Allow the seed pods to dry and turn brown on the plant, then harvest the seeds. | Store in a cool, dry place in a labeled envelope or container. |
| Squash | Allow the fruit to mature and turn brown, then remove and dry the seeds. | Store in a cool, dry place in a labeled envelope or container. |
| Strawberries | Allow the fruit to mature and turn dark red, then remove and dry the seeds. | Store in a cool, dry place in a labeled envelope or container. |
| Sweet Corn | Allow the ears to mature and dry on the plant, then remove and dry the kernels. | Store in a cool, dry place in a labeled envelope or container. |
| Sweet Potato | Allow the seed balls to mature and turn brown on the plant, then harvest them. | Store in a cool, dry place in a labeled envelope or container. |
| Swiss Chard | Allow the plant to flower and the seeds to dry on the stalk. | Store in a cool, dry place in a labeled envelope or container. |
| Tomato | Remove the seeds from a ripe tomato, then rinse and dry them. | Store in a cool, dry place in a labeled envelope or container. |
| Oregano | Allow the seed heads to dry on the plant, then harvest the seeds. | Store in a cool, dry place in a labeled envelope or container. |
| Zucchini | Allow the fruit to mature and turn yellow, then remove the seeds. | Rinse and dry the seeds, then store in a cool, dry place in a labeled envelope or container. |

# Chapter 24: Conclusion

*"Gardening simply does not allow one to be mentally old, because too many hopes and dreams are yet to be realised."*

– Allan Armitage

Well, we have finally made it to the end. I am confident that you now have a great understanding of what is required to grow your own food in a garden, raised bed, or container.

I expect that when you started this journey you were a little unsure what would be involved and whether you had the skills required. But now after all these pages, I know you have learned that all you really need is some soil, some light, some water, and a few seeds and you can easily grow your own garden.

Take some time to reflect on what we have covered, as there has been a great deal of information presented in these pages. Re-read what you need and think about it. You have all the skills you need, even if you don't believe me.

So, go get some soil, find a suitable place to grow your plants, and get your hands dirty. This book will be there to help you through the rough spots and give you some inspiration when you are looking to take the next step.

Happy gardening.

# References

*3 Victory Garden Plans to Get Gardening!* (n.d.). Almanac.Com. Retrieved December 23, 2022, from https://www.almanac.com/victory-garden-plans

*6 Gourmet Salad Recipes by Michelin-Star Chefs.* (n.d.). Retrieved December 23, 2022, from https://www.finedininglovers.com/article/gourmet-salad-recipes

*7 Types of Manure to Use on Your Garden | Pip Magazine.* (n.d.). Retrieved January 6, 2023, from https://pipmagazine.com.au/grow/types-of-manure/

*8 Surprising Health Benefits of Gardening | UNC Health Talk.* (2020, May 18). https://healthtalk.unchealthcare.org/health-benefits-of-gardening/

*9 of the Worst Mulching Mistakes That Are Easy to Avoid.* (n.d.). Better Homes & Gardens. Retrieved January 28, 2023, from https://www.bhg.com/gardening/yard/mulch/mulching-mistakes-to-avoid/

*10 most Common Plant Pests | C-I-L® Lawn and Garden.* (n.d.). Retrieved February 3, 2023, from https://www.cillawnandgarden.com/en/tips/indoor-gardening-planters-and-flower-bed/10-most-common-plant-pests

*13 Best Flowers for Attracting Pollinators to the Garden | Gardener's Path.* (n.d.). Retrieved January 31, 2023, from https://gardenerspath.com/plants/flowers/best-flowers-for-pollinators/

*16 Ways to Use Companion Planting for Pest Control Naturally.* (n.d.). Retrieved January 30, 2023, from https://thefreerangelife.com/companion-planting-to-control-pests-naturally/

*20 Vegetables to Never Grow Together + Ideas for Companion Vegetables.* (n.d.). Retrieved January 30, 2023, from https://www.tasteofhome.com/collection/vegetables-you-should-never-grow-together-plus-companion-vegetables/

*…21 …31 …41 …* (n.d.). Retrieved December 23, 2022, from http://cf-galaxy.com/en/article/planet-food/29-21-31-41-

*35 Inspiring Gardening Quotes to Encourage You to Grow Plants.* (n.d.). Retrieved January 19, 2023, from https://ecowarriorprincess.net/2020/05/best-inspiring-gardening-quotes-grow/

*544 Vermiculite Stock Photos—Free & Royalty-Free Stock Photos from Dreamstime.* (n.d.). 544 Vermiculite Stock Photos - Free & Royalty-Free Stock Photos from Dreamstime. Retrieved January 10, 2023, from https://www.dreamstime.com/photos-images/vermiculite.html

*A FREE 160 page book of wartime Ministry of Food leaflets. – The 1940's Experiment.* (n.d.). Retrieved December 22, 2022, from https://the1940sexperiment.com/2020/04/30/a-free-160-page-book-of-wartime-ministry-of-food-leaflets/

*A Homeowner's Guide to Fertilizer.* (n.d.-a). Retrieved January 11, 2023, from https://www.ncagr.gov/cyber/kidswrld/plant/label.htm

*A Homeowner's Guide to Fertilizer.* (n.d.-b). https://www.ncagr.gov/cyber/kidswrld/plant/label.htm

*A Michelin-Starred Veggie Stock.* (n.d.). Food Network. Retrieved December 23, 2022, from https://www.foodnetwork.com/healthyeats/recipes/2016/10/a-michelin-starred-veggie-stock

*About Pollinators.* (n.d.). Pollinator.Org. Retrieved January 31, 2023, from https://www.dev.pollinator.org/pollinators

*Albert Howard Quote.* (n.d.). A-Z Quotes. Retrieved January 19, 2023, from https://www.azquotes.com/quote/552057

*Assorted gardening tools leaning on white wall photo – Free Garden tools Image on Unsplash.* (n.d.). Retrieved December 23, 2022, from https://unsplash.com/photos/z70ocusaJcw

*Beginners Guide to Companion Planting—Heeman's.* (n.d.). Retrieved January 30, 2023, from https://www.heeman.ca/garden-guides/companion-planting/

*Benefits of Having a Family Garden.* (n.d.). Verywell Family. Retrieved December 20, 2022, from https://www.verywellfamily.com/family-garden-to-improve-health-4127202

*Birds | Pests & Diseases | Thompson & Morgan.* (n.d.). Retrieved February 3, 2023, from https://www.thompson-morgan.com/pests/birds

*Bowled over: California turns out a bounty of lettuce and leafy greens | The Packer.* (n.d.). Retrieved December 18, 2022, from https://www.thepacker.com/news/produce-crops/bowled-over-california-turns-out-bounty-lettuce-and-leafy-greens

C, J. (2013, June 19). *25 Fruits And Vegetables To Grow In Acidic Soil.* Off The Grid News. https://www.offthegridnews.com/survival-gardening-2/25-fruits-and-vegetables-to-grow-in-acidic-soil/

celcook. (2017, December 29). The Accidental Invention of the Microwave | commercial microwave. *Celcook.* https://celcook.ca/the-accidental-invention-of-the-microwave/

Choosing the right fertilizer. (2010, March 14). *Johntheplantman--Gardening.* https://johntheplantman.com/2010/03/14/choosing-the-right-fertilizer/

*Coco Coir as a Growing Medium.* (n.d.). Aqua Gardening. Retrieved January 10, 2023, from https://www.aquagardening.com.au/learn/coco-coir-growing-medium/

*Commercial Soil Testing.* (n.d.). Retrieved January 11, 2023, from https://soilhealth.osu.edu/soil-health-assessment/commercial-soil-testing

*Companion Planting | West Coast Seeds.* (n.d.). Retrieved January 30, 2023, from https://www.westcoastseeds.com/blogs/garden-wisdom/companion-planting

*Companion Planting for Pest Control—The Beginner's Garden.* (n.d.). Retrieved January 30, 2023, from https://journeywithjill.net/gardening/2019/02/26/companion-planting-pest-control/

*Compost Physics—Cornell Composting.* (n.d.). Retrieved January 10, 2023, from https://compost.css.cornell.edu/physics.html

*Deter Pests Naturally by Companion Planting With These Super Flowers—Garden Therapy.* (n.d.). Retrieved January 30, 2023, from https://gardentherapy.ca/flowers-deter-pests/

*Determining DLI (Daily Light Integral) from PAR | Onset's HOBO and InTemp Data Loggers.* (n.d.). Retrieved December 28, 2022, from https://www.onsetcomp.com/resources/tech-notes/determining-dli-daily-light-integral-from-par

Dibble, L. (2021, September 21). What Is A Victory Garden—Vintage Advice for a Modern Time. *Hillsborough Homesteading.* https://hillsborough-homesteading.com/victory-garden-free-pdf/

*Differentiating Cotyledons (First Leaves) from True Leaves – Gardyn Help Center.* (n.d.). Retrieved January 19, 2023, from https://mygardyn.zendesk.com/hc/en-us/articles/4412114901901-Differentiating-Cotyledons-First-Leaves-from-True-Leaves

*Discover How to Feast Year-Round From a Small Garden!* (n.d.). Abundant Mini Gardens. Retrieved December 20, 2022, from https://abundantminigardens.com/how-much-money-can-you-save/

*DLI Calculator | SunTracker Technologies Ltd.* (n.d.). Retrieved December 28, 2022, from https://www.suntrackertech.com/dli-calculator/

Domoney, D. (2016, February 26). 35 inspirational gardening quotes and famous proverbs David Domoney. *David Domoney.* https://www.daviddomoney.com/35-inspirational-gardening-quotes-and-famous-proverbs/

*Eight quotes that illustrate why water is life ᐅ – Your Connection to Wildlife.* (n.d.). Retrieved January 13, 2023, from https://blog.cwf-fcf.org/index.php/en/8-quotes-that-illustrate-why-water-is-life/

*Electromagnetic Spectrum—Introduction.* (n.d.). Retrieved December 27, 2022, from https://imagine.gsfc.nasa.gov/science/toolbox/emspectrum1.html

Ellis, A. (n.d.). *The victory garden guide.*

*Favorite Gardening and Landscaping Quotes.* (2014, October 10). Best Buy In Town Landscape Supply. https://www.bestbuyintown.biz/2014/10/10/favorite-gardening-landscaping-quotes/

*Fertilizer, Dung, Compost, Mulch—Quotes, Sayings, and Wisdom for Gardeners.* (n.d.). Retrieved January 19, 2023, from https://gardendigest.com/fert.htm

*Fertilizing the Vegetable Garden—7.611.* (n.d.). Extension. Retrieved January 11, 2023, from https://extension.colostate.edu/topic-areas/yard-garden/fertilizing-the-vegetable-garden-7-611/

Flowers, F. (2012, June 26). *Which type of manure is best for your garden? | Canadian Living.* https://www.canadianliving.com/home-and-garden/article/which-type-of-manure-is-best-for-your-garden

GARDENING. (2022, February 8). 171 Inspirational Gardening Quotes And Sayings. *Backyard Boss.* https://www.backyardboss.net/171-inspirational-gardening-quotes-and-sayings/

*Gardening ebook: Ministry of Agriculture Allotment and Garden Guides—1945.* (n.d.). Retrieved December 22, 2022, from http://www.earthlypursuits.com/AllotGuide/AllotGuide.htm

*Germination | Description, Process, Diagram, Stages, Types, & Facts | Britannica.* (n.d.). Retrieved January 17, 2023, from https://www.britannica.com/science/germination

*Get to know your potting mix: Vermiculite and perlite—The Washington Post.* (n.d.). Retrieved January 5, 2023, from https://www.washingtonpost.com/lifestyle/home/get-to-know-your-potting-mix-vermiculite-and-perlite/2014/03/25/c0385bf2-add0-11e3-b8b3-44b1d1cd4c1f_story.html

Government of Canada, C. C. for O. H. and S. (2022, December 23). *Shovelling: OSH Answers.* https://www.ccohs.ca/oshanswers/ergonomics/shovel.html

*Grandpa's Victory Garden.* (n.d.). Retrieved December 22, 2022, from https://www.cityfarmer.org/grandpasVG.html

*Green City Growers | Urban Farming | 10 Reasons to Grow Your Own Food.* (n.d.). Retrieved December 18, 2022, from https://greencitygrowers.com/blog/10-reasons-to-grow-your-own-food/

*Green light: Is it important for plant growth?* (n.d.). MSU Extension. Retrieved December 27, 2022, from https://www.canr.msu.edu/news/green_light_is_it_important_for_plant_growth

*Green plant on white and purple floral ceramic pot photo – Free Waste Image on Unsplash.* (n.d.). Retrieved January 10, 2023, from https://unsplash.com/photos/FTCQPjPfFS4

*Growing Under the Spruce Tree—Salisbury Greenhouse.* (n.d.). Retrieved January 28, 2023, from https://salisburygreenhouse.com/under-the-spruce-tree/

*Growing vegetable gardens near black walnut trees.* (2016, April 22). MSU Extension. https://www.canr.msu.edu/news/growing_vegetable_gardens_near_black_walnut_trees

*Growing Vegetables: Asparagus [fact sheet].* (2018, January 17). Extension. https://extension.unh.edu/resource/growing-vegetables-asparagus-fact-sheet

*Hardening Off Seedlings.* (n.d.). West Coast Seeds. Retrieved January 25, 2023, from https://www.westcoastseeds.com/blogs/garden-wisdom/hardening-off-seedlings

*Hardiness Zones in Australia.* (n.d.). Gardenia.Net. Retrieved December 22, 2022, from https://www.gardenia.net/guide/australian-hardiness-zones

*Hardiness Zones of Europe.* (n.d.). Gardenia.Net. Retrieved December 22, 2022, from https://www.gardenia.net/guide/european-hardiness-zones

*History of USDA Plant Hardiness Zone Maps—The Rest of the Story.* (n.d.). Retrieved December 22, 2022, from https://www.plantdelights.com/blogs/articles/plant-hardiness-zone-maps

*How Much Does a Soil Test Cost?* (n.d.). Angi. Retrieved January 11, 2023, from https://www.angi.com/articles/how-much-does-testing-soil-cost.htm

*How to attract pollinators—David Suzuki Foundation.* (n.d.). Retrieved January 31, 2023, from https://davidsuzuki.org/living-green/how-to-attract-pollinators/

*How to Grow a Three Sisters Garden.* (2016, May 27). Native-Seeds-Search. https://www.nativeseeds.org/blogs/blog-news/how-to-grow-a-three-sisters-garden

How to Grow Asparagus. (n.d.). *Heeman's*. Retrieved January 4, 2023, from https://www.heeman.ca/garden-guides/how-to-grow-asparagus/

*How To Increase The pH In Soil?* (2022, July 18). Atlas Scientific. https://atlas-scientific.com/blog/how-to-increase-the-ph-in-soil/

*How to Plan a Vegetable Garden: A Step-by-Step Guide*. (n.d.). GrowVeg. Retrieved December 20, 2022, from https://www.growveg.com/guides/how-to-plan-a-vegetable-garden-a-step-by-step-guide/

*How to Transplant Seedlings Outdoors | MiracleGro Canada*. (n.d.). Retrieved January 23, 2023, from https://miraclegro.com/en-ca/landscaping-planning/how-to-transplant-seedlings-outdoors.html

*How to Use Perlite to Improve Soil and Boost Plant Growth – Garden Betty*. (n.d.-a). Retrieved January 5, 2023, from https://www.gardenbetty.com/perlite/

*How to Use Perlite to Improve Soil and Boost Plant Growth – Garden Betty*. (n.d.-b). https://www.gardenbetty.com/perlite/

*Inspriational & Famous Garden Quotes | Install-It Direct*. (n.d.). Retrieved January 19, 2023, from https://www.installitdirect.com/learn/garden-quotes/

*Introducing the Concept of DLI to the World—Fluence*. (n.d.-a). Retrieved December 28, 2022, from https://fluence-led.com/science-articles/introducing-the-concept-of-dli-to-the-world/

*Introducing the Concept of DLI to the World—Fluence*. (n.d.-b). Retrieved December 28, 2022, from https://fluence-led.com/science-articles/introducing-the-concept-of-dli-to-the-world/

*Jesus-era seed is the oldest to germinate | New Scientist*. (n.d.-a). Retrieved January 18, 2023, from https://www.newscientist.com/article/dn14125-jesus-era-seed-is-the-oldest-to-germinate/

*Jesus-era seed is the oldest to germinate | New Scientist*. (n.d.-b). https://www.newscientist.com/article/dn14125-jesus-era-seed-is-the-oldest-to-germinate/

Jonas, S., & News ·, K. O. · C. (2022, November 11). *Lettuce fans tossed by soaring prices, leading to expensive salads, substitutions | CBC News*. CBC. https://www.cbc.ca/news/canada/montreal/romaine-lettuce-shortage-montreal-restaurant-1.6648798

Keenan, G. (2021, April 9). 21 Grow Your Own Food Quotes for a Healthier You This 2022. *Guy About Home*. https://www.guyabouthome.com/21-grow-your-own-food-quotes-for-a-healthier-you-this-2021/

Knox Seed Company & Henry G. Gilbert Nursery and Seed Trade Catalog Collection. (1943). *Garden guide, 1943: Garden for victory*. Stockton, California : Knox Seed Company. http://archive.org/details/CAT31361789

Konstantinides, A. (n.d.). *10 easy soup recipes Michelin-starred chefs love making in the winter*. Insider. Retrieved December 23, 2022, from https://www.insider.com/easy-winter-soup-recipes-from-michelin-starred-chefs-2020-12

*Lancaster New Era 31 Mar 1943, page 4*. (n.d.). Newspapers.Com. Retrieved January 13, 2023, from https://www.newspapers.com/image/560914974/

*Lead Pipes Threaten the Drinking Water of Millions of City Residents | by Stephen Bell | Age of Awareness | Medium*. (n.d.). Retrieved January 13, 2023, from https://medium.com/age-of-awareness/lead-pipes-in-nyc-are-you-at-risk-9b7e078672a0

*Light Quotes (3884 quotes)*. (n.d.). Retrieved January 19, 2023, from https://www.goodreads.com/quotes/tag/light

Ltd, B. (n.d.). *Tree Growing Out Of Abandoned Car 2 Free Stock Photo—Public Domain Pictures*. Retrieved January 10, 2023, from https://www.publicdomainpictures.net/en/view-image.php?image=252154&picture=tree-growing-out-of-abandoned-car-2

May 02, & Palmer, 2022 Brian. (n.d.). *A World Without Bees? Here's What Happens If Bees Go Extinct*. NRDC. Retrieved February 3, 2023, from https://www.nrdc.org/stories/world-without-bees-heres-what-happens-if-bees-go-extinct

MeganCain. (2013, March 21). *How to Germinate Seeds Successfully Every Time*. Creative Vegetable Gardener.

https://www.creativevegetablegardener.com/how-to-germinate-seeds/

*Michelin Star Salad: Gourmet Salad Recipes—Fine Dining Lovers*. (n.d.). Retrieved December 23, 2022, from https://www.finedininglovers.com/article/gourmet-salad-recipes

*Most produce loses 30 percent of nutrients three days after harvest – Chicago Tribune*. (n.d.). Retrieved December 18, 2022, from https://www.chicagotribune.com/dining/ct-xpm-2013-07-10-chi-most-produce-loses-30-percent-of-nutrients-three-days-after-harvest-20130710-story.html

Nutrition, C. for F. S. and A. (2023). Lead in Food, Foodwares, and Dietary Supplements. *FDA*. https://www.fda.gov/food/environmental-contaminants-food/lead-food-foodwares-and-dietary-supplements

*Organic Mulch A Complete Guide [Pick The Best Natural Mulch]*. (2019, June 7). https://simplysmartgardening.com/best-organic-mulch/

*Parts of a Flower: An Illustrated Guide | AMNH*. (n.d.). Retrieved February 2, 2023, from https://www.amnh.org/learn-teach/curriculum-collections/biodiversity-counts/plant-identification/plant-morphology/parts-of-a-flower

Paz, M., Fisher, P. R., & Gómez, C. (2019). Minimum Light Requirements for Indoor Gardening of Lettuce. *Urban Agriculture & Regional Food Systems*, *4*(1), 190001. https://doi.org/10.2134/urbanag2019.03.0001

*Periodic Graphics: The elements of fertilizers*. (n.d.). Chemical & Engineering News. Retrieved January 13, 2023, from https://cen.acs.org/food/agriculture/Periodic-Graphics-elements-fertilizers/98/i11

*Perlite Beneficiation Process*. (n.d.). Retrieved January 10, 2023, from https://www.911metallurgist.com/blog/perlite

*Photo by Jonathan Cooper on Pexels*. (n.d.). Pexels. Retrieved January 10, 2023, from https://www.pexels.com/photo/bags-stones-and-bucket-on-ground-12247008/

*Photo by Skitterphoto on Pexels*. (n.d.). Pexels. Retrieved January 14, 2023, from https://www.pexels.com/photo/spraying-of-water-on-plants-730923/

*Plants That Naturally Repel Aphids—Controlling Aphids With Plants*. (n.d.-a). Retrieved January 30, 2023, from https://www.gardeningknowhow.com/plant-problems/pests/insects/plants-that-repel-aphids.htm

*Plants That Naturally Repel Aphids—Controlling Aphids With Plants*. (n.d.-b). https://www.gardeningknowhow.com/plant-problems/pests/insects/plants-that-repel-aphids.htm

*Richard Brinsley Sheridan Quotes*. (n.d.). BrainyQuote. Retrieved January 19, 2023, from https://www.brainyquote.com/quotes/richard_brinsley_sheridan_120428

Risk of lead poisoning from urban gardening is low, new study finds. (n.d.). *UW News*. Retrieved January 13, 2023, from https://www.washington.edu/news/2016/02/02/risk-of-lead-poisoning-from-urban-gardening-is-low-new-study-finds/

*Salt Resistant Gardens: Plants That Tolerate Salty Soil*. (n.d.-a). Retrieved January 13, 2023, from https://www.gardeningknowhow.com/special/seaside/gardening-salt-water-soil.htm

*Salt Resistant Gardens: Plants That Tolerate Salty Soil*. (n.d.-b). https://www.gardeningknowhow.com/special/seaside/gardening-salt-water-soil.htm

SanSone, A. (2021, March 25). *Different Types of Plants and Flowers That'll Attract Pollinators to Your Garden*. The Pioneer Woman. https://www.thepioneerwoman.com/home-lifestyle/gardening/g35927657/best-pollinator-plants/

Schiller, N. (2022, January 1). *23 Beneficial Insects & Creepy Crawlies Great for Your Garden*. Gardener's Path. https://gardenerspath.com/how-to/disease-and-pests/beneficial-insects/

*Seed Quotes Quotes (127 quotes)*. (n.d.). Retrieved January 19, 2023, from https://www.goodreads.com/quotes/tag/seed-quotes

Shaw, J. (2018, July 30). *Do Evergreens Change the pH Balance of Your Soil?* Trees Unlimited. https://treesunlimitednj.com/do-evergreens-change-the-ph-balance-of-your-soil/

ShipABCO. (2018, October 26). *Shipping Fresh Produce: What You Need to Know.* ABCO Transportation. https://www.shipabco.com/shipping-fresh-produce-what-you-need-to-know/

*Shovel Rake Dirt—Free photo on Pixabay.* (n.d.). Retrieved December 23, 2022, from https://pixabay.com/photos/shovel-rake-dirt-farm-garden-1867123/

*Shovel Tool Garden—Free vector graphic on Pixabay.* (n.d.). Retrieved December 23, 2022, from https://pixabay.com/vectors/shovel-tool-garden-hardware-30627/

*Sinigang "best rated" vegetable soup in the world.* (n.d.). Retrieved December 23, 2022, from https://www.cnnphilippines.com/videos/2021/8/4/Sinigang--best-rated--vegetable-soup-in-the-world.html

*Soil Management.* (n.d.). Retrieved December 30, 2022, from https://www.ctahr.hawaii.edu/mauisoil/a_comp.aspx

Staff, T. com. (2020, April 26). *11 Different Types of Shovels (Anatomy, Uses & Pictures).* Trees.Com. https://www.trees.com/gardening-and-landscaping/types-of-shovels

*The Best Watering Cans of 2023, Tested in Our Lab.* (n.d.). Retrieved January 15, 2023, from https://www.realsimple.com/home-organizing/gardening/best-watering-cans

*The Human Eye Can See Infrared Light, Plus 5 Other Things You Had No Idea Eyes Can Do | Insight Eye Specialists—Utah LASIK and Cataract Doctors.* (2015, November 19). https://www.insighteyespecialists.com/the-human-eye-can-see-infrared-light-plus-5-other-things-you-had-no-idea-eyes-can-do/

*The Most Popular Vegetables Grown in American Backyards.* (n.d.). SeedsNow.Com. Retrieved December 22, 2022, from https://www.seedsnow.com/blogs/news/14694693-the-most-popular-vegetables-grown-in-american-backyards

Tools, D. (n.d.). *Ten Quotes About Tools to Inspire Greatness.* Defiance Tools. Retrieved January 19, 2023, from https://www.defiancetools.com/blogs/guides/ten-quotes-about-tools-to-inspire-greatness

*Top 20 Garden Vegetables to Grow | Kellogg Garden Organics™.* (n.d.). Retrieved December 22, 2022, from https://kellogggarden.com/blog/gardening/top-20-garden-vegetables-to-grow/

Torres, A. P., Lopez, R., Horticulture, P., & Architecture, L. (n.d.). *Measuring Daily Light Integral in a Greenhouse.*

*Transplant shock—What triggers it and how to protect plants against die-off.* (n.d.-a). Retrieved January 25, 2023, from https://www.nature-and-garden.com/gardening/transplant-shock.html

*Transplant shock—What triggers it and how to protect plants against die-off.* (n.d.-b). https://www.nature-and-garden.com/gardening/transplant-shock.html

*Transporting food generates whopping amounts of carbon dioxide.* (n.d.). Retrieved December 18, 2022, from https://www.nature.com/articles/d41586-022-01766-0

*Types of Fertilizer—Gardening Solutions—University of Florida, Institute of Food and Agricultural Sciences.* (n.d.). Retrieved January 11, 2023, from https://gardeningsolutions.ifas.ufl.edu/care/fertilizer/types-of-fertilizer.html

*Types Of Inorganic Mulch—Benefits And Disadvantages Of Inorganic Mulch.* (n.d.-a). Retrieved January 27, 2023, from https://www.gardeningknowhow.com/garden-how-to/mulch/using-inorganic-mulch-in-gardens.htm

*Types Of Inorganic Mulch—Benefits And Disadvantages Of Inorganic Mulch.* (n.d.-b). https://www.gardeningknowhow.com/garden-how-to/mulch/using-inorganic-mulch-in-gardens.htm

*Types of Mulch and Why You Should Use Them.* (n.d.). The Spruce. Retrieved January 26, 2023, from https://www.thespruce.com/what-is-mulch-1402413

*Types Of Soil—Sandy Soil, Clay Soil, Silt Soil, And Loamy Soil*. (n.d.). BYJUS. Retrieved December 30, 2022, from https://byjus.com/biology/types-of-soil/

*United States Plant Zone Map | PlantAddicts.com*. (n.d.). Retrieved December 22, 2022, from https://plantaddicts.com/united-states-plant-zone-map/

University, U. S. (n.d.). *Storing Canned Goods*. Retrieved December 26, 2022, from https://extension.usu.edu/preserve-the-harvest/research/storing-canned-goods=

*Unusual Salad Greens that aren't lettuce*. (n.d.). Retrieved December 15, 2022, from https://gardentherapy.ca/unusual-salad-greens/

*USDA plant hardiness zone map: [United States]*. (n.d.). [Image]. Library of Congress, Washington, D.C. 20540 USA. Retrieved December 22, 2022, from https://www.loc.gov/resource/g3701d.ct003970/

*Vegetable Container Gardening for Beginners*. (n.d.). The Spruce. Retrieved December 15, 2022, from https://www.thespruce.com/vegetable-container-gardening-for-beginners-848161

*Vegetable Crop Soil pH Tolerances—Harvest to Table*. (n.d.). Retrieved January 28, 2023, from https://harvesttotable.com/vegetable-crop-soil-ph-tolerances/

*Vegetable Garden Layout: 7 Best Design Secrets! - A Piece Of Rainbow*. (n.d.). Retrieved December 22, 2022, from https://www.apieceofrainbow.com/vegetable-garden-layout-design-ideas/

*Victory Gardens | The Canadian Encyclopedia*. (n.d.-a). Retrieved December 21, 2022, from https://www.thecanadianencyclopedia.ca/en/article/victory-gardens

*Victory Gardens | The Canadian Encyclopedia*. (n.d.-b). Retrieved January 13, 2023, from https://www.thecanadianencyclopedia.ca/en/article/victory-gardens-editorial

*Victory Gardens—For family and country. A thriving Victory Garden—Not on an island, but in a London bomb crater, close to Westminster Cathedral. Where the Nazi's sowed death, a Londoner and his wife have sown life-giving vegetables*. (1943, January 1). [Image]. Library of Congress. https://loc.getarchive.net/media/victory-gardens-for-family-and-country-a-thriving-victory-garden-not-on-an-54a947

*Visible Light | Science Mission Directorate*. (n.d.). Retrieved December 27, 2022, from https://science.nasa.gov/ems/09_visiblelight

*Water Sources | Public Water Systems | Drinking Water | Healthy Water | CDC*. (2022, April 6). https://www.cdc.gov/healthywater/drinking/public/water_sources.html

*What Are Cotyledons, Monocots, and Dicots?* (n.d.). The Spruce. Retrieved January 19, 2023, from https://www.thespruce.com/what-are-cotyledons-monocots-and-dicots-1403098

*What Are the Best Light Sources For Photosynthesis?* (2018, September 4). Vernier. https://www.vernier.com/2018/09/04/what-are-the-best-light-sources-for-photosynthesis/

*What is Photosynthesis |*. (n.d.). Retrieved December 27, 2022, from https://ssec.si.edu/stemvisions-blog/what-photosynthesis

*What is the Best Mulch? Benefits and Drawbacks of Various Mulch Materials*. (2013, March 21). New Garden Landscaping & Nursery | Landscape, Design & Garden Centers. https://newgarden.com/notes/what-is-the-best-mulch

*What Science Reveals About A Child's Lovey or Security Blanket—Preschool Inspirations*. (n.d.-a). Retrieved January 26, 2023, from https://preschoolinspirations.com/security-blanket-loveys/

*What Science Reveals About A Child's Lovey or Security Blanket—Preschool Inspirations*. (n.d.-b). https://preschoolinspirations.com/security-blanket-loveys/

*What to Plant in a Victory Garden*. (n.d.). Almanac.Com. Retrieved December 21, 2022, from https://www.almanac.com/what-plant-victory-garden

*What Would Happen If All the Bees Died? | Britannica*. (n.d.-a). Retrieved February 3, 2023, from https://www.britannica.com/story/what-would-happen-if-all-the-bees-died

*What Would Happen If All the Bees Died? | Britannica*. (n.d.-b). https://www.britannica.com/story/what-would-happen-if-all-the-bees-died

*Which Type of Water is Best For Your Vegetable Garden? -.* (2019, May 29). https://nelsonwater.com/blog/type-water-best-vegetable-garden/

*Why Conventional Lettuce Can Take Up To Two Weeks Longer Than Bowery From Seed To Store—Bowery Farming.* (n.d.). Retrieved December 18, 2022, from https://boweryfarming.com/why-conventional-lettuce-can-take-up-to-two-weeks-longer-than-bowery-from-seed-to-store/

*Why do we consume only a tiny fraction of the world's edible plants?* (n.d.). World Economic Forum. Retrieved December 15, 2022, from https://www.weforum.org/agenda/2016/01/why-do-we-consume-only-a-tiny-fraction-of-the-world-s-edible-plants/

*Why More And More People Have Begun Growing Their Own Food.* (n.d.). Retrieved December 18, 2022, from https://www.tastingtable.com/889482/why-more-and-more-people-have-begun-growing-their-own-food/

*Will Compost Burn Plants? Tips for Using Compost on Plants – Backyard Sidekick.* (n.d.-a). Retrieved January 5, 2023, from https://backyardsidekick.com/will-compost-burn-plants-tips-for-using-compost-on-plants/

*Will Compost Burn Plants? Tips for Using Compost on Plants – Backyard Sidekick.* (n.d.-b). https://backyardsidekick.com/will-compost-burn-plants-tips-for-using-compost-on-plants/

*World's Most Famous Salads.* (2020, April 29). Erudus. https://erudus.com/editorial/the-food-agenda/worlds-most-famous-salads

www.ingramcontent.com/pod-product-compliance
Lightning Source LLC
Chambersburg PA
CBHW040533020526
44117CB00028B/18